BERLIN

The Buildings of Europe

BERLIN

Derek Fraser

Manchester University Press

Manchester and New York

Distributed exclusively in the USA by St. Martin's Press

Copyright © Derek Fraser 1996

Published by
Manchester University Press
Oxford Road, Manchester M13 9NR, UK
and
Room 400, 175 Fifth Avenue,
New York, NY 10010, USA

Distributed exclusively in the USA by
St. Martin's Press, Inc.,
175 Fifth Avenue, New York, NY 10010, USA

British Library Cataloguing-in-Publication data
A catalogue record for this book is available from
the British Library

Library of Congress-Cataloging-in-Publication data

Fraser, Derek.
  The buildings of Europe : Berlin / Derek Fraser.
  p. cm..
  Includes index.
  ISBN 0–7190–4021–3. – ISBN 0–7190–4022–1
  1. Architecture–Germany–Berlin. 2. Berlin (Germany)–Buildings. structures. etc. I. Title.
NA1085.F73 1997
720'.9431'55–dc20   96-31546 CIP

ISBN 0 7190 4021 3 hardback
ISBN 0 7190 4022 1 paperback

First published 1996

00 99 98 97 96   10 9 8 7 6 5 4 3 2 1

Typography by Nick Loat

Layout by Christopher Woodward

Printed in Great Britain by
Redwood Books, Trowbridge, Wiltshire

How to Use this Guide

There are 184 entries: buildings, engineering structures, parks and residential estates, arranged in chapters geographically. The reference number of each entry is used on the maps at the back of the guide to show its location. On visiting Berlin it is advisable to acquire a detailed city map for the accurate pinpointing of locations using the addresses given in the guide. Visits will be easier if you use Berlin's excellent, integrated public transport system: S-Bahn (suburban trains), U-Bahn (underground trains) and buses. Distances can be great, so forward planning and careful selection will help make the most of any given opportunity. The visitor to Berlin is well served with information. Popular magazines like Check-Point and Berlin turns on carry information on the city's activities, events and exhibitions. The Berlin Tourist Office is located in the Europa Centre 28, and regular architectural exhibitions are held in the Berlin Pavilion 43, Martin-Gropius-Bau 76 and the Staatsratsgebäude 7.

The inclusion of a building in this guide does not mean its grounds or interior are accessible to the public. Please respect the privacy of those living or working in the buildings listed.

Contents

Quadriga, Brandenburg Gate

Introduction

Berlin lies on the great plain of the North German flatlands, the Mark Brandenburg. Located in the centre of Europe it served as a crossroads for the main trade routes between north and south, east and west. Earlier this century, it grew to become one of Europe's great cities, vying with London and Paris, its population reaching 4.3 million at the outbreak of the Second World War in 1939. Growth over the last half-century has been relatively slow from the city's post-war depletion of 2.8 million to its present 3.5 million.

In area, however, the city remains Germany's largest, covering 889 square kilometres (343 square miles), extending 38 Kilometres (24 miles) from north to south and 45 Kilometres (28 miles) from east to west. It is large enough to contain the combined areas of Munich, Stuttgart and Frankfurt. The contrasting cityscape is surprisingly varied; inner-city apartment blocks of Kreuzberg open out to the secluded villas and leafy suburbs of Zehlendorf, and the commercial vibrancy of the new western centre is a world apart from the romantic landscape of the Peacock Island on Lake Havel. Surprisingly, one-third of the land within the city limits consists of parks, forests, lakes and waterways.

By comparison with other major cities Berlin is relatively young, having celebrated its 750th anniversary in 1987. It first became capital of Prussia in

New western centre

Neues Palais, Sanssouci 180

Introduction

1815 before becoming capital of the newly established German Empire in 1871. Since that period of great expansion, social unrest, and housing reforms at the turn of the century, the city has experienced turbulent times. Infiation, depression, tyranny, war, defeat, isolation and division have all left their mark. Berliners, therefore, have become a tough breed. With intellectual and cultural dynamism, they have evolved their cosmopolitan little island behind the Iron Curtain into a most vibrant and exciting city. Traditionally liberal and tolerant, they often display a love of the provocative and unconventional. Their quick repartee and sardonic humour is apparent by the nicknames chosen for so many of the city's buildings and landmarks.

Evolution and change are necessary if a city is to avoid becoming a museum piece. Berlin has endured more than most and now more fundamentally has a unique opportunity to reinvent itself. In 1987 the fall of the Berlin Wall, shown on newscasts around the world, came to symbolise the decline of Communism. German unification in 1990 was followed later by Berlin regaining its capital status. The speed at which such major changes have occurred has left many of the consequences of partition yet to be overcome. With the social divisions between East and West likely to remain for some time longer, it is interesting to note that a dual society also existed back in the early years of the city's origins.

The Electors

The twin communities of Kölln and Berlin developed at the narrowest crossing point of the River Spree, half-way between the fortresses of Spandau and Köpenick. This strategic route, with at first a ford and then a bridge, connected the fishermen on a sandy island with the merchants on the right bank. The 1987 anniversary commemorated the first written records dating back to 1237, with the 'union' of Berlin and Kölln following in 1307, resulting in the construction of a joint town hall.

The political and economic growth was engineered by the Margraves of Brandenburg by a shrewd policy of customs duties which encouraged trade via Berlin. The town was invited to join the Hanseatic League - Europe's first Common Market - in 1359, and, together with this powerful confederation of Baltic towns, continued to prosper despite the destruction caused by the great fire of 1380. The Zollerns, originally Swabian overlords, became the Burgraffen of Nuremberg through marriage and took the grander name of Hohen-Zollern. In 1414, Margrave Friedrich of Hohen-Zollern joined forces with the town to recover territory seized by two marauding barons, Johann and Dietrich Quitzow. A year later, the Emperor granted Friedrich the hereditary title to the March of Brandenburg which brought its holder also the dignity of Elector.

It was left to the first Elector's successor, Elector Friedrich II to establish a town palace on the island of Kölln in 1443. Subsequent limitation of the citizens' privileges by this new authority resulted in an uprising which was quickly repressed by the Elector and finally secured the future of the twin towns as the electoral Capital. This new establishment of the Elector's officials and courtiers set the tone of urban life and attracted numerous noblemen to town. The increasing demand for utility goods and luxury articles drew many craftsmen to town and from 1450 until 1600 the population of 6,000 doubled to 12,000. The original palace eventually proved too small to accommodate all the public authorities, courtiers and officials. Under Elector Joachim II, a larger site was established, outwith municipal control, with the master builders Krebs and Theyss starting work on a Renaissance building in 1538. Drawings show an elaborately decorated four-storey building with stair towers wide enough for riders on horseback and an elevated bridge link to the court church. The building was not completed until around 1600 and formed the basis of the Stadtschloss which occupied the area known as Schlossplatz (until recently Marx-Engels-Platz).

The Great Elector, Friedrich Wilhelm of Brandenburg, 1640–88, proved to be a great commander and considerable administrator. Influenced by having spent much of his youth in Holland, he built quays along the banks of the Spree and constructed a canal between the Spree and the Oder to stimulate commerce. One of his most influential acts, following the devastation of the Thirty Years War in 1648 with the population reduced to 7,500, was to encourage immigration. The Huguenots (Calvinists) fleeing from Louis XIV's Catholic France were encouraged to settle in Berlin with the Edict of Potsdam in 1685. Although granted the right to self-government, the Huguenots' influence on economic life, administration, education, arts and sciences cannot be underestimated. It is recorded that the refugees introduced some forty-six new trades and founded the first Academy of Arts in 1694.

Designated as a garrison town, from 1658 a massive star-shaped fortification was constructed to enclose Berlin, Kölln and Friedrichswerder with an eight-metre high wall, moat, thirteen bastions and six gates. An important route

Introduction

Schloss Charlottenburg 118

from the main west gate to the Elector's Country Palace through the hunting grounds of the Tiergarten had been established as early as 1573. This avenue 'under the limes', Unter den Linden, laid out more formally in the 1650s became the major east-west axis for setting off future expansion. Even before the fortifications were finished in 1683, Johann Arnold Nering was called upon to lay out Dorotheenstadt (1674, named after the Great Elector's new wife Dorothea) to the north of the Linden and the later more important Friedrichstadt (1688), to the south. Nering employed a strict gridiron plan creating only one major square in Friedrichstadt - the Gendarmenmarkt (formely Platz der Akademie).

The Kings of Prussia

The Elector Friedrich III crowned himself Friedrich I, King of Prussia in 1701. As the royal capital of Brandenburg-Prussia, Berlin developed throughout the eighteenth century into an important political, economic, and cultural centre. During his period as the Elector, Friedrich III had the Stadtschloss altered and extended as a Baroque palace in 1698–1716 by Andreas Schülter. In 1845–53 a dome was added by Friedrich August Stüler based on an idea by Karl Friedrich Schinkel. The war-damaged remains were pulled down in 1950–51 with one of the portals incorporated into the Staatsratsgebäude 7 which now occupies part of the site. Friedrich III also established a new country palace, Schloss Charlottenburg 118, for his Queen Sophie-Charlotte in 1695.

After his succession to the throne, Friedrich Wilhelm I (1713–40) was compelled to economise since his father had depleted the treasury. He was

Town plan 1826

less interested in embellishing the town than making it more powerful by expanding and increasing the fortifications. This was a period of strict moral standards and a spartan way of life for both the Court and the citizens. He earned the nickname 'The Soldier King' by introducing a policy of systematic recruitment which became the basis of Prussian military power.

The construction in 1736 of the 'Linie', a 14 kilometre long customs wall with fourteen gates, established a new boundary with enough land to contain the additional suburbs until the late nineteenth century. Nering's Friedrichstadt plan was expanded to the south-west by Philipp Gerlach between 1732 and 1738 sufficiently far to establish three new public spaces against the boundary of the Linie. The Quarré, the Rondell and the Oktogon, identifiable by their contrasting geometry, provided monumental squares inside the gates. In the north, the 'square', Pariser Platz, created a forecourt to the early Brandenburg Gate which led to the Tiergarten and the Charlottenburg Palace **118**, while to the south the 'circus', Belle-Alliance-Platz (now Mehringplatz),

Introduction

served Hallesches Gate and in the middle the 'octagon', Leipziger Platz, lay before the Potsdam Gate which led to Potsdam and the Sanssouci Palace **177**.

From the Rondell in the south radiated three major streets in a northerly direction. In the centre was Friedrichstrasse, forming the north-south axis and bisecting the Linden at right angles to connect with Dorotheenstadt. The north-west street (now Wilhelmstrasse) connected to the Linden at the Brandenburg Gate and the street to the north-east (now Lindenstrasse) connected with the Friedrichswerder quarter of the old town. This plan with its network of geometry represents one of the most interesting examples of a seventeenth century Baroque urban design. By comparison to the more organic form of the medieval town, it imposed an order by which future development could be controlled. The tree-lined avenue, in the tradition of north European landscape design, became one of the recurring features of Berlin's urban planning as the expansion eventually continued out and beyond the old town bastions.

Friedrich II (Frederick the Great), came to the throne in 1740 during the period of 'The Enlightenment' of which he was both an admirer and exponent. It was also a period of great military activity with the Silesian Wars, the Seven Years War and the partition of Poland establishing Prussia as a great power. The intellectual views of Immanuel Kant and Georg W. F. Hegel encouraged a dutiful, spiritual and philosophical view of life. Friedrich II developed his own artistic interests, both as a composer and performer of music, and in 1776 founded the *Ecole de Génie et d'Architecture*. He influenced the architectural

Bebelplatz

direction of Berlin from Baroque to Neo-Classical and, inspired by ancient Greece, constructed various monumental buildings along the Unter den Linden, including the Forum Fridericianum (now Bebelplatz), and established the summer palaces on the edge of the Brandenburg forests and lakes at Potsdam. Before his death in 1786, Berlin had acquired St Hedwig's Cathedral 18 by Johann Boumann, the Old Library 20, by Georg Christian Unger, the Opera House 19 and the Sanssouci Palace 177 by Georg Wenzeslaus von Knobelsdorff.

Under Friedrich Wilhelm II (1786–97) the continuing growth of Prussian power with its analogy to ancient Greece is aptly illustrated by the construction of the Brandenburg Gate 25 in 1789 by Carl Gotthard Langhans. Marking the main ceremonial entry to the city, inspiration for this triumphal arch came from the Propylaea on the Acropolis in Athens. The classical legacy of Friedrich the Great was also developed through the visionary projects of Friedrich Gilly and from 1797, under the reign of Friedrich Wilhelm III (1797–1840), by the works of his pupil, Karl Friedrich Schinkel. In this age of enlightenment it is Schinkel, the 'universal man', who best expresses the spirit of the age in architecture. The educated bourgeoisie hungry for progress looked to the ideas of Greco-Roman antiquity as social models for the new Prussian state. The philosophers, August and Friedrich Schlegel idealised the classical antiquity of ancient Greece as a state in perfect harmony with its earthly surroundings. Delight in nature became a popular theme explored by the arts in general. Caspar David Friedrich painted idealised landscapes of mountains, forests, oceans and ruins dramatically lit by moonlight, dawn or sunset. Ludwig van Beethoven first performed his 6th Symphony, the 'Pastoral', in 1808.

Schinkel, 'the image of genuine humanity', was driven by a conviction that a new Prussian society would best be realised through its architecture. In 1815, his promotion to Oberbaurat (Senior Adviser) by the King enabled him to prepare and execute in an official capacity the commissions which so decisively characterised his work in Berlin. The Neue Wache 16 (1816–18) beside the Zeughaus 15 and the Altes Museum 10 (1823–28) opposite the Stadtschloss amongst others led to the development of Classicism in Germany. In 1820, Schinkel was appointed professor of architecture and a member of the senat of the Akademie der Künste and his influence continued when, in 1830 he was promoted to the rank of Oberbaudirektor in charge of Prussia's building programme. His responsibilities extended to bridges,

Introduction

conservation work and environmental improvements and his design talents ranged from stage sets for Mozart's operas to Berlin's street signs. Crown Prince Friedrich Wilhelm (IV) was a willing patron and collaborator and, together with the royal director of gardens Peter Joseph Lenné, contributed to Schinkel's best works of Romantic Classicism which can be found on the Havel lakeside estates and in Potsdam.

Following a Prussian defeat in the Battle of Jena-Auerstedt, Napoleon marched into the city in 1806 and Berlin endured two years of French occupation. Wilhelm von Humboldt, working in the Prussian Ministry of the Interior, founded the Friedrich Wilhelm University 21 in 1810 located in the former palace of Prince Heinrich (Friedrich II's brother) on Unter den Linden. After Napoleon was defeated at Waterloo in 1815 power was restored and the German Federation was created at the Congress of Vienna. Berlin benefited from its growing prestige and continued to grow as an important centre of trade and industry. With new cotton, wool and silk industries established, Berlin in 1750 had become the largest textile town in Germany. By 1800 the population reached 200,000 and the town was the third largest in Europe after London and Paris. In the early nineteenth century the textile, porcelain and iron industries were joined by numerous machine tool factories. In 1838, August Borsig, the 'Locomotive King' founded a heavy engineering plant and the railway line between Berlin and Potsdam was opened.

With his accession to the throne, would-be architect Friedrich Wilhelm IV (1840–61) promoted the industrial exhibition of 1844 which demonstrated the impressive status the city had attained. Such phenomenal growth also created social and political tensions with the deterioration of living conditions for the men, women and children being employed in the mechanised factories. The increasing demand for housing led to land speculation, exorbitant rents and homelessness. Growth was largely restricted to the area within the old customs wall and areas such as Friedrichshain, Kreuzberg and Lichtenberg were compressed to oversaturation with an average of seventy-two people per building plot. Political rallies and street fighting led to the 'March Revolution' of 1848. The royal interventions proved unsuccessful and resulted in the imposition of martial law by General von Wrangel. The Prussian government proclaimed an 'Imposed Constitution' which remained in force until 1918, and included an undemocratic three-class franchise as part of the municipal code.

Apartment block, Kreuzberg

Although the first building regulations introduced in 1853 required obligatory fire protection between dwellings, they still permitted an extremely high density and the overdevelopment of the courtyards behind the street frontage. City architect and engineer, James Hobrecht produced a plan in 1862 for extending the city in a concentric form. Although it promoted wide avenues and new drainage, it contained few squares and parks. Hobrecht supported the social mix found in the cross-section of the typical apartment block resulting from the varying rents asked for ground, upper, attic and courtyard apartments. The social and political benefits of this system were preferred to the 'English' model of herding the rich and poor into separate areas of the city.

The German Emperors

During the reign of Wilhelm I (1861–67) Otto von Bismark served as the Chancellor and Foreign Minister of Prussia from 1862 until 1871 when he became the first Chancellor of the German Empire which his policies had helped to create. Wilhelm I was then proclaimed Kaiser (Emperor) in the Hall of Mirrors in Versailles and Berlin became the capital of Germany, the Second German Reich. With this promotion to the rank of imperial capital the population explosion continued, reaching one million by 1877, one and a half million by 1890 and two million just after the turn of the century. The new national unity, however, did not include the political freedom fought for by the people in 1848. The Imperial Insurance Office was formed as a controlling authority of employee and unemployment insurances and the first Social Insurance Acts in the 1880s marked the beginning of national measures to improve the workers' conditions. The lifestyle of the poor and underprivileged was

Introduction

captured in the cartoons and caricatures of Heinrich Zille whose sharp wit and social criticisms made him a regular contributor to the satirical journals of the day.

During the age of Kaisers Wilhelm I (1871–88) and Wilhelm II (1888–1918) new local and long-distance transport networks were built, linking the metropolitan area with neighbouring communities such as Charlottenburg, Wilmersdorf and Schöneberg. A westward shift took place in developing new urban districts for the middle and upper bourgeoisie. Admiration for the conquered city of Paris and the further implementation of the Hobrecht plan led to the creation of palatial apartment blocks and fine new avenues with the Kurfürstendamm reflecting the urban elegance of the Champs-Elysées. This period of confidence and imperial sabre-rattling often produced large-scale ornate architecture such as the Reichstag **26** (1884–95) by Paul Wallot, and the Viktoria Insurance Headquarters **88** (1906–13) by Wilhelm Walther in a style dubbed by critics as 'Reich braggadocio'. Berlin also attained international repute as a city of science, museums, theatre and music.

The Weimar Republic

Following Germany's military defeat in 1918, hunger and war-weariness, compounded with political unrest, culminated in mass strikes and the November revolution. Kaiser Wilhelm II abdicated, Friedrich Ebert was named Reich Chancellor, Philipp Scheidemann of the SDP proclaimed the 'German Republic'

Apartment block, Tiergarten

and Karl Liebknecht of the Spartacus Union the 'Free Socialist Republic'.
Political instability brought power struggles and numerous large-scale strikes
culminating in a currency depreciation of grotesque proportions. The city's
boundaries were reorganised to amalgamate metropolitan Berlin and its
ninety-three surrounding urban and rural municipalities. This 'Greater Berlin'
was subdivided into twenty administrative districts which exist up to the
present day, and created the second largest city in Europe after London.
Now the largest industrial city on the continent, the major commercial,
banking and stock exchange centre, the most important railway junction and
the second largest inland port, Berlin became the 'air junction of Europe'
when the Tempelhof Airport **112** was first opened in 1924. Two years later,
the film-maker Fritz Lang released his masterpiece *Metropolis*.

During the 1920s general improvements of political and economic conditions
encouraged further growth and the city gained an international reputation as
an intellectual and cultural centre. Albert Einstein was awarded the Nobel
Prize in 1921 and Erich Mendelsohn's Einstein Tower **175** in Potsdam was
completed three years later. Artists such as Max Beckmann, George Grosz
and Raoul Hausmann were at the centre of Berlin's avant-garde. A whole
entertainment industry sprang up with thirty-five playhouses, twenty concert
halls and several opera houses. The theatre flourished under Max Reinhardt
and Bertolt Brecht produced his *Threepenny Opera* in 1928. Radio Berlin
broadcast Germany's first programmes in 1923 with television broadcasts

Siedlung Britz **130**

Introduction

following six years later. The film industry won international acclaim thanks to directors such as Fritz Lang, Ernst Lubitsch, Carl Mayer and stars like Emil Jannings and Marlene Dietrich. This expanding industry, by its very nature extrovert and creative, fostered the development of new building types exemplified by the Cinema Universum, 1928, part of Mendelsohn's Woga Complex on the Kurfürstendamm **37**.

The Bauhaus, founded in 1919 in Weimar by Walter Gropius, was relocated to its new buildings in Dessau in 1925. It was in Berlin, however, that many of its ideals were put into practice. Along with hotels, cafés, department stores and restaurants, over 100,000 housing units were built. For modern architecture and urban design, Berlin became a world focus for international debate. Here could be found the works of Walter Gropius, Ludwig Mies van der Rohe, Hans Scharoun and the expressionists Hans Poelzig and Erich Mendelsohn. With a tendency to reject history and inner-city deprivation, the modernists' concerns with providing daylight, fresh air and sunlight led to many peaceful, green field housing estates 'Siedlungen' in areas such as Zehlendorf **151** and Britz **130** by Bruno Taut, Hugo Häring and others. Housing co-operatives and trade union construction syndicates ensured an acceptable standard for workers' housing.

The National Socialists

As the golden 1920s gave way to the depression of the 1930s, the National Socialist party led by Adolf Hitler grew from strength to strength. Mass unemployment, soaring tax and utility rates combined with pay cuts drove many to the radical political parties with political killings and street fighting becoming features of public life. The burning of the Reichstag and the appointment of Hitler as Chancellor in 1933 ensured that the principle of totalitarianism replaced municipal self-government. The book burning in the Opera Square and the discrimination against the Jews led to the emigration of many politicians, scientists, artists and architects. The Bauhaus, having relocated in Berlin in 1932, was closed by the authorities after operating for barely one year. Modern architecture was dismissed as cosmopolitan and degenerate, forcing many of its exponents to seek employment abroad. The 'Heimatstil' (Romantic Vernacular) was favoured in place of the 'Neue Sachlichkeit' (New Objectivity) except for large public buildings where a spartan Classicism was preferred, unfortunately lacking Schinkel's proportional delicacy.

The outwardly impressive Olympic Games of 1936 were designed to turn attention away from the problems of unemployment and poor standards of living. The following year Albert Speer was charged with reshaping Berlin to create the new world capital of 'Germania'. The building priorities changed from serving the individual to planning government, military and diplomatic buildings to serve the party. Speer's unrealised masterplan consisted of a five kilometre long avenue forming a new north-south axis fronted on both sides by about fifty important buildings of enormous scale. The large public square in the south was linked to a railway station to the west and Tempelhof Airport 112 to the east. From this assembly point, the world-conquering German armed forces would march northwards along the triumphal route which culminated in a domed assembly building of vast proportions. Modelled on Hitler's sketches, this new 'Pantheon' would have been over five times as high and contained sixteen times the volume of the original. The demolition of entire districts was halted by the outbreak of war in 1939, limiting the damage to the area around today's Cultural Forum and the Spreebogen area near the Reichstag 26.

The occupied city

For Berlin, the Second World War ended in May 1945, having been subjected to numerous allied bombing raids and the systematic destruction by the Red Army. The legacy bequeathed to the city by the 'Thousand Year Reich' included 80,000 dead and seventy-five million cubic metres of debris. Within greater Berlin, one-fifth of the buildings were completely destroyed or beyond repair with the highest concentration around the historic centre. That summer after signing the 'Potsdam Accord' the Soviets were joined by the British, American and the French who entered the city as occupying powers. Municipal sovereignty was divided into four sectors and under the control of the Red Army, a new Berlin Magistrature was established.

Hans Scharoun was appointed as director of the Building and Housing Department. Fundamental reconstruction plans were produced following modernist principles of urban development, the loosely structured city ideas of Le Corbusier. There was never any plan to repair, upgrade or preserve the tenement city which, in accordance with the modernist view had a negative association with the past. Instead they looked to the 'Siedlungen' (residential estates) of the 1920s with developments like Siemensstadt, Britz and Onkel-Toms-Hütte. The works of the Tauts, the Luckhardts, Gropius and Scharoun became the yardstick for planners. Ironically while the 'Collective Plan', a

Introduction

reconstruction programme developed by Scharoun in 1946, was delayed because of shortages of building materials, the 'Zehlendorfer Plan' which dealt with facilitating transport and communications resulted in clearing the rubble and rehabilitating the damaged building stock.

Contrasting approaches to rehousing the population by the Allies and the Soviets can be seen in the Hansaviertel in the West and Stalinallee (now Karl-Marx-Allee/Frankfurter Allee) in the East. The Interbau Exhibition **43**, announced in 1953 and opened in 1957, redeveloped the Hansaviertel on the edge of the Tiergarten. The strategy adopted the anti-street polemic of the Congrès Internationaux d'Architecture Moderne (CIAM) (1928) in creating a dispersed arrangement of individual buildings by international architects, integrated into a green landscape. The National Reconstruction Programme of the East followed the Moscow Building Conference edict of 1954, 'to build more, more quickly and more cheaply'. Despite, therefore, having to adapt prefabricated, industrialised building techniques, Stalinallee adopted a more urban strategy by creating a wide avenue leading into the elliptical space of Strausberger Platz **5**, with references to much of Berlin's earlier architecture.

The political division of the city in 1948 started when the Soviets withdrew from the Four Power administration organisation. The currency reforms and the Berlin blockade led to the formation in 1949 of the German Federal

The Wall at Potsdamer Platz, 1987

IBA reconstruction: new apartments near the wall 79

20

New western centre

World Clock, Alexanderplatz

Republic and the German Democratic Republic. The popular uprising of 1953 and its suppression by the Eastern authorities contributed towards the influx of refugees to the West, and in 1961 the 'Wall' **77** was built.

The divided city

With its economy incorporated in the Marshall Plan, Western money was available to transform West Berlin into the 'window of the free world': a blatant display of wealth to demonstrate what capitalism and free enterprise could achieve. A new 'Western' centre developed around the Zoo Bahnhof **33** and along the Kurfürstendamm with the Kaiser Wilhelm Memorial Church **27** as a focal point, a contrived ruin uncharacteristically left as a poignant reminder of the war. Most of the recent surrounding architecture is incoherent and anonymous with a predominance of neon signs and commercial curtain walling.

The old town centre, now in the East, had almost been totally destroyed by the war. A new Alexanderplatz was constructed during the 1960s as a new city centre showpiece - a forum for the German Democratic Republic - with the Television Tower **3** intended as a 'progressive' symbol to mark the authority of Democratic Socialism over the city. As an urban space it suffers from vast proportions, ill-defined edges and the visual disharmony of building bland concrete high-rise housing beside the renovated Berlin Rathaus (Town Hall) **1** and the Marien Church **2**.

In the West, however, most of the building activity was transferred to the outskirts of the city with the old, inner-city residential districts being demolished or simply neglected. The construction of new roads and motorways largely determined the course of urban development, often ignoring the original city ground plan. Political confusion brought a halt to most inner-city building with the exception of the 'cultural belt' project on the banks of the Spree between Museumsinsel and Charlottenburg Palace **118**. The central

Introduction

focus of this idea was the 'Kulturforum' (Cultural Forum) **48** laid out by Hans Scharoun on a site cleared by Speer near Kemperplatz. It was here that Scharoun sited his Philharmonic Hall **49** (1960–63) and Mies returned from the United States to see the completion of his National Gallery **53** (1965–68).

Political and economic stability returned with the Quadripartite Agreement of 1971 which facilitated and safeguarded the ties between East and West Berlin. An economic recession during the late 1970s brought a rapid decline in building and the city's political and social problems escalated in the rehabilitated housing areas. Priorities changed and, in line with other major cities, a need was identified to replace demolition and incoherent redevelopment by the conservation and reconstruction of existing urban districts. With this background, the Internationale Bauausstellung (IBA) was established in 1979.

With the motto 'the inner city as a place to live' the IBA organised a building programme of 'critical reconstruction' and 'careful urban renewal' under the directorship of Josef Paul Kleihues and Hardt-Waltherr Hämer. Specific areas were identified: the Tegel Harbour in the north, Prager Platz in Wilmersdorf and the much larger concentration of areas in southern Tiergarten, southern Friedrichstadt, and Luisienstadt next to the Wall.

Gendarmenmarkt

An enormous amount of work has been initiated by the IBA with hundreds of feasibility studies and architectural competitions involving collaborations with public authorities and private developers. Although much of the work involved Berlin and German architects, many international figures have contributed projects including some better known as architectural 'theorists'. Despite the constraints, the organisers have been prepared to experiment and engage in the wider debate by creating an international laboratory of contemporary architecture within an historic city context.

The majority of this work was planned for completion in 1987 to coincide with Berlin's 750th anniversary celebrations. Following the official end of IBA, continuity was assured with the 'renewal' work being taken over by a private successor organisation STERN and the 'reconstruction' by the Senate Building and Housing Department.

During this period, work was also undertaken in the East to restore a number of important buildings, badly damaged during the war. In the old centre, the Rathaus 1 and the Dom 9 have been rebuilt along with buildings on the Museuminsel. The restoration of the Nikolai Church 6 (1977–87) has included the rebuilding of the surrounding buildings which, despite using modern construction, recapture the scale and character of this old quarter. Schinkel's Schauspielhaus 22 and the twin churches 23 in Gendarmenmarkt (formerly Platz der Akademie) have been successfully restored to recreate a showpiece of Berlin's Romantic Classicism.

The future capital

The fall of the Wall in 1989, the political and administrative reunification in 1990 and the decision taken in 1991 by the German Bundestag to restore Berlin as the seat of parliament and government will all be significant factors in shaping the city's future. Four major projects presently focus on the centre of the city. The Reichstag 26 is being restored to its original purpose by Sir Norman Foster, the result of a limited international competition. Work has commenced on developing Potsdamer Platz 56. Its pivotal position linking the new western centre with the old city centre together with its historic importance led to much public debate. The prize-winning urban design by Hilmer and Sattler involves building designs by many international architects including new headquarters for Daimler-Benz by Renzo Piano and the Sony headquarters by Murphy and Jahn. The Spreebogen, with a master plan by Schutes and Frank, will create a new government district on the banks of the

Introduction

Apartment block in the former east

Spree adjacent to the Reichstag **26**. The fourth competition deals with the transformation of Alexanderplatz, centre of the historic city and heart of the former German Democratic Republic.

With the demolition of the Wall, many of the IBA projects which dealt with the 'edge' of the Western city have become 'central' to the unified city. The urbar design concept of 'mending the city' takes on a new meaning when faced witl the problems created by the open scar of 'no man's land'. Many of the new initiatives will focus on the former East with plans to renovate a large propor- tion of the old housing stock (around 170,000 traditional apartments and 270,000 panel-system high-rise units). Sites have also been designated around the city for 90,000 new housing units and 7.5 million square metres of commercial space with the necessary ancillary facilities such as nurseries, schools and training colleges.

For a city covering an area similar to that of London or Paris with less than half the population, Berlin is bound to enter another era of significant growth. Many businesses and institutions are presently engaged in relocating their operations to the city with, no doubt, many others considering the possibility. The present building boom worth thousands of millions of Deutschmarks includes a wide diversity of projects, with a concentration of prominent architects from Germany and abroad, unparalleled in any other city. Such intensive building activity and international involvement inevitably brings up th question of Berlin's future character.

Hans Stimmann, the Senatsbaudirektor, had set the guidelines for the critical reconstruction by specifying building heights, density and mix. Although the historic building lines and historic street pattern of roads and squares must be respected or reconstructed, these regulations make no explicit statements about the architecture. The intention is to strengthen the identity of the city by encouraging both home-based and international architects to respect the historic context and time-tested traditions and develop them further by using their own individual creative and interpretative qualities. Traditionally, Berlin displayed a tolerance for innovative ideas, often encouraging and promoting new architectural movements. It remains to be seen, however, if this belief in the experimental promise of architecture will assist Berlin in attaining its goal: to become *the* European metropolis of the next millennium.

Kranzler Restaurant, Kurfürstendamm

Office building 1994, Helmut Jahn 36

View from the Schlossbrücke

Old town centre and northern Friedrichstadt

1 Berliner Rathaus (Berlin Town Hall)
1861–69

Rathausstrasse 15–18, Jüdenstrasse 1–3,
Mitte

Hermann Friedrich Waesemann

In the early years, Berlin and Kölln retained separate administrations, the former with two Burgomasters and ten Councillors and the latter with exactly half that number. Having decided to combine their strengths in the 'Union' of 1307, the joint council built a third town hall at the Lange Brücke (now Rathausbrücke). The present town hall, built in a High Renaissance style with a 97 metre high tower and containing three courtyards, is a building of immense style and imposing character. It would appear well suited to its change of status when, only two years after its completion, Berlin was promoted to the rank of imperial capital with the establishment of the Second Reich. The history of the city until the foundation of the empire by Bismark in 1871 can

be seen depicted on thirty-six red terracotta panels forming a frieze dating from ten years after the building's completion. The building gets its nickname 'Rotes Rathaus' (Red Town Hall) from the red clinker brickwork typical of the Brandenburg area.

The fountains by Reinhold Begas, relocated here after the war, originally sat in front of the nearby Stadtschloss (demolished 1950–51).

2 Marienkirche (Marien Church)
from 1380

Karl-Liebknecht-Strasse 8, Mitte

This is one of the original parish churches of Berlin and has undergone many alterations over the past seven centuries. Now sitting rather uncomfortably and exposed on the vast new Alexanderplatz, the original building was started circa 1270 and then rebuilt after the great fire of 1380. The vestibule was added in 1418. The high tower above it is by Steffen Boxthude of 1466; its neo-Gothic upper section is by Carl Gotthard (1789). The surrounding street pattern at right angles to the River Spree still reflects the plan of the medieval town which conflicted with the east-west orientation of its churches. The town centre plan of 1877 shows the church sitting across the diagonal axis of a perimeter block, open only along its north side to the road.

Old town centre and northern Friedrichstadt

3 Fernseh und UKW Turm (Television Tower)
1965–69
Panoramastrasse, Mitte
Fritz Dieter, Günter Franke

Rising from the centre of Alexanderplatz to a height of 365 metres, the TV Tower is a visual marker for the old town centre. Constructed during the era of the Wall as a symbol for East Berlin and Democratic Socialism, the tower was visible from most of West Berlin, thereby providing a constant reminder of the East-West division. Around the base, a cluster of festive pavilions house various exhibitions and the Berlin Information Centre, their ferro-concrete roofs rising and dipping like giant folded paper fans. The Tower itself, by contrast, is more austere with its tapering shaft finished in untreated *in situ* concrete. The metal clad observation globe contains two panoramic viewing platforms and a restaurant which revolves once per hour. From this elevation of 207 metres, it is possible to appreciate the changes to the grain of the city below with its heterogeneous mixture of old and new.

4 Berolinahaus and Alexanderhaus: office and commercial Buildings 1928–31
Alexanderplatz 1–2, Mitte
Peter Behrens

The buildings resulted from an urban design competition which also attracted proposals from Ludwig Mies van der Rohe, Martin Wagner and the Luckhardts.

The planning geometry is generated by two major considerations: forming a gateway to Rathausstrasse on one side and responding to the elliptical form of the original Alexanderplatz on the other. Both buildings are connected visually by the expression of two glazed staircases which when illuminated at night represent variations on the 'glass tower' theme. With shops occupying the ground, the reticulated façade on the upper storeys consistently repeats a double square reinforced concrete panel with square windows subdivided into squares. The design, considered at the time to be a masterpiece of 'Neue Sachlichkeit' (New Objectivity), has proved influential to the work of other architects particularly some of the recent rationalists.

5 Haus Berlin and Haus des Kindes: Residential and Commercial Building
1951–53

Strausberger Platz 1 and 19, Mitte

Herman Henselmann, Rolf Göpfert, Emil Leibold

These twin towers form a gateway to the elliptical Strausberger Platz which acts as a hinge in the slight bend of Karl-Marx-Allee. Their strong composition of stepped and overlapping volumes owes much to the early skyscrapers of the 1920s. Looking east the long vista of the avenue is visually terminated by Henselmann's twin towers of Frankfurter Tor which in turn are modelled on Gontard's eighteenth-century church towers 23 in the Gendarmenmarkt. Henselmann fully exploits the potential of the East German industrialised building techniques by introducing a high level of detail articulation, a considered use of proportion and strong geometric form to create one of the most powerful urban spaces built in Eastern Europe since the end of the war. Unfortunately, this quality of design is not echoed by the other slab blocks and high-rise buildings along the avenue where boring repetition and wide mastic joints predominate. It is interesting to contrast this work with the approach taken in planning the Hansaviertel 43 built on the edge of the Tiergarten between 1955 and 1957.

6 Nikolaikirche (Nicolai Church)
from 1380 with additions in 15th century

Poststrasse, Mitte

Recognisable by its distinctive twin spires, the Nicolai Church is the oldest parish church in Berlin. Started as a late Romanesque stone basilica *circa* 1230, the church was rebuilt later that century as an early Gothic hall church and, after the fire of 1380, it was again rebuilt. Additional chapels were added *circa* 1400, with the nave and the lady chapel added in 1452. The neo-Gothic tower with twin spires was added in 1876 to a design by Hermann Blankenstein. Although the building was badly damaged during the Second World War it was rebuilt in 1977–87 and now serves as a museum and concert hall.

The church serves as a focal point to the Nicolai quarter where the surrounding buildings have been rebuilt to follow the old street pattern. Successful as this may be in terms of scale and capturing something of the atmosphere of 'old Berlin', there is, however, a visual conflict between the use of traditional wrought ironwork, hanging shop signs and cobbled streets with the system built concrete construction of the new buildings.

Old town centre and northern Friedrichstadt

**7 Portal IV des Berliner Stadtschlosses
(Town Palace Portal IV)** 1706–13

Schlossplatz (ex Marx-Engels-Platz), Mitte

*Andreas Schülter, Johann Friedrich von
Eosander*

The Berliner Stadtschloss (the Berlin Royal Palace) was demolished by the Communist regime in 1950–51 after being badly damaged during the Second World War. The Staatsratsgebäude (State Council Building) which occupies part of the palace site was built in 1962–64, and designed by Roland Korn and Hans-Erich Bogatzky. It incorporates the reconstruction of the fourth portal from the Palace built between 1698 and 1716 to designs by Andreas Schülter and his successor Eosander. It was from the balcony of this portal that Karl Liebknecht proclaimed the new German Socialist Republic during November 1918, an occasion which the Communist authorities felt worthy of immortalising. Although beautifully restored with its original sculptural decoration the portal sits uncomfortably, located off-centre, on the modern façade facing Schlossplatz (formerly Mark-Engels-Platz).

8 Palast der Republik 1973–76

Schlossplatz (Marx-Engels-Platz), Mitte

Heinz Graffunder, Karl-Ernst Swora

A headquarters for the old Communist regime, the building was closed following German unification in 1990. The site was first occupied by a stronghold built by the Elector Friedrich II in 1443. Under Joachim II this was transformed into a Renaissance building by Caspar Theyss in 1538. It was further extended as a Baroque palace in 1698–1716 to the designs of Andreas Schülter and Johann Friedrich von Eosander. Friedrich August Stüler added a dome in 1845–53, based on an idea by Karl Friedrich Schinkel, and into the 1930s no building in the city centre was allowed to exceed the height of the lantern on top. There are those in Berlin who would like to see the palace reconstructed. The present 'Republican Palace' (former home of the East German parliament) forms the eastern extremity of Schlossplatz (formerly Marx-Engels-Platz) with its 180 metre long façade. When in use the spacious interior contained various foyers and viewing galleries with a restaurant and cafeteria looking east over the River Spree towards the Television Tower **3** on Alexanderplatz and west over the neatly parked rows of Trabants in Marx-Engels-Platz. The building's status called for a prestigious physiognomy which involved the use of white marble and reflective tinted glass. Nicknamed the 'House of a Thousand Windows', the building's future is now somewhat in doubt.

9 Dom (The Cathedral) 1894–1905
Schlossplatz (Marx-Engels-Platz), Mitte
Julius Carl, Otto Raschdorff

The original cathedral built on this site in 1747 was rebuilt by Schinkel in 1817, adjacent to his later Altes Museum **10** forming two sides of the Lustgarten. The present neo-Renaissance building resulted from a national competition and served as the principal Protestant church for both state and court. The crypt contains the tombs of the Great Elector, Friedrich I and his wife Sophie Charlotte. Badly damaged during the Second World War it has been slowly rebuilt ever since, the four corner domes without their lanterns and the large dome with a much reduced lantern. Built during the era of the Second Reich, the new building seems pompous, overscaled and stylistically at odds with its remaining ninententh century neighbours.

10 Altes Museum 1823–28
Lustgarten, Mitte
Karl Friedrich Schinkel

The idea of arranging the finest art treasures in the kingdom within one building came originally from a public lecture in 1797 by Alois Hirt (later to teach at Schinkel's Bauakademie). Nine years, later following a collaboration between Hirt and Schinkel on an art exhibition, the idea became official policy. The collection, while under the aegis of the king, would be housed in a public museum rather than within the palace. The French Wars had made the obligatory Grand Tour of Italy difficult and therefore a chronological assembly of art works would benefit not only artists and scholars but have a 'civilising' effect on the public. It was Schinkel's involvement in building the Schlossbrücke **14** and alterations to the cathedral which led to the creation of an urban space in the Lustgarten, or pleasance, to the north of the Great Elector's palace. It is a tribute to the understanding of King Friedrich Wilhelm III for accepting the brilliant concept of creating a purpose-built museum facing the northern side of the palace, thus completing the new square which terminated the 'Linden'. Extensive works were carried out in draining the marshy ground and altering the water courses to create the area now known as Museumsinsel (Museum Island).

Schinkel gives the building a monumental dignity by extending a wide peristyle across the entire façade and raising it on to a solid podium which related more in scale to the cathedral, Stadtschloss and Zeughaus **15**. The podium, apart from also providing a barrier from the moist soil, was designed to contain service rooms for

staff, scholars and artists lit by basement windows on the north, east and west sides. The plan geometry was derived from Durand's 'Précis' (1802–09), which illustrated permutations of modular plan types. This utilitarian and typological inspiration is given life in a spatial articulation of enormous power and delicacy. The rectangular two-storey structure, enclosing two courtyards and a central drum, presents a broad inviting frontage to the Lustgarten. Reached by a wide flight of steps, an impressive row of eighteen Ionic columns, stopped at each end by antae, creates a long 'Vorhalle', or stoa, for displaying mural paintings by Schinkel (completed by others after his death in 1841 and since destroyed). A five-bay opening with four more columns leads to the entrance vestibule.

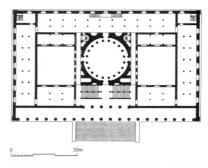

The central space, a domed rotunda based on the Pantheon, was where the most treasured antique statues and busts were displayed. The space is articulated by a series of Corinthian columns supporting a circular gallery, the soffit of which, like the underside of the dome, was originally coffered. In the post-war reconstruction, the diameter of the drum was reduced at the lower level under the balcony resulting in tighter dimensions and a loss of the coffers. On either side of the rotunda, galleries of varying sizes are symmetrically disposed around the two courtyards, but it is the central space and the double winged staircase immediately in front of it which best illustrate the genius of Schinkel. Concealment of the dome to the exterior maximises the drama and impact of its discovery to the interior. The staircase not only connects the ground and upper floor but opens up the interior of the building to the vestibule and offers delightful views through the Ionic columns on to the Lustgarten, an extraordinary dematerialisation of interior and exterior space. Unfortunately, the full effect of this extraordinary sequence has been partly reduced by the recent insertion of a glazed screen set between the Ionic columns.

The collection, in two historic parts, was regarded as representing the fundamental roots of European civilisation: Greco-Roman sculpture on the ground and Renaissance painting on the level above. The sculptural ornamentation designed by Schinkel consists of eighteen Prussian eagles above the entablature, four female figures holding candelabras at the corners of the building and four mythical figures holding rearing horses on the cubic surrounds to the rotunda. The two equestrian statues on the open staircase are by August Kiss and Hubert Wolff. The great bowl of polished red granite in front of the building was hewn out of a single piece of local ice-age stone by Christian Gottlieb Cantian and was originally intended as a centrepiece in the rotunda.

11 Nationalgalerie 1866–76
Bodestrasse, Mitte
Friedrich August Stüler, Johann Heinrich Strack

The site to the north of the Altes Museum **10**, the most northern area of Kölln, was designated by Friedrich Wilhelm IV in 1841 as an area dedicated to art and antiquity. This so-called 'Museumsinsel' (Museum Island) saw the development of several museum buildings up until the 1930s. Stüler, a gifted pupil of Schinkel, built the Neues Museum in 1843–55 (thereby designating Schinkel's museum the 'Altes') to the rear of the older building and linked by a bridge connection.

This was followed by the National Gallery designed by Stüler and built by Strack in the form of a Roman temple raised on a two-storey plinth. A broad double-winged staircase rises up to the portico with an equestrian statue of the king by Alexander Calandrelli (1897) in front of it. The buildings, along with the others on Museum Is- land, were badly damaged during the Second World War. The National Gallery has been successfully restored and work is continuing on the Neues Museum.

12 Pergamonmuseum 1912–30
Am Kupfergraben, Mitte
Alfred Messel, Ludwig Hoffmann

The museum contains a collection of Oriental and Greco-Roman antiquities, a market gate from Miletus, and the most valued cultural treasure, the Pergamon Altar.

The excavations of Pompeii from the mid eighteenth century stimulated a great interest in antiquities with many expeditions receiving royal sponsorship. The acquisition of the altar from the acropolis at Pergamon in the Ottoman Empire (now Turkey) was regarded as a national success and its arrival in Berlin was celebrated by a festival attended by crowds in ancient costumes. Dating from 180–159 BC the altar was built as a triumphal monument and consecrated offering to Pergamon's goddess of protection, Athena. The sculptured marble frieze is a fine example of the Hellenistic school and the colonnades are said to have influenced the work of Albert Speer. Unfortunately, the rather dingy setting in the present building lacks the intensity of Mediterranean light and presents the work like a set for a Cecil B. de Mille film.

Old town centre and northern Friedrichstadt

13 Bodemuseum 1898–1904

Monbijoubrücke, Mitte

Ernst von Ihne

Located on the most northerly point of Kölln and reached by the arched Monbijoubrücke, the Bodemuseum occupies a prominent waterfront site. The triangular ground plan, containing no less than five courtyards, is organised about a central axis with its apex curved to the fork in the river and crowned by a dome. Built in a neo-Baroque style, the continuous rhythm of classical articulation and the sculpted figures along the parapet hark back to Berlin's earlier palaces. The building is home to the Egyptian collection, fifteenth to eighteenth century paintings, primeval and early history, and the coin collection.

14 Schlossbrücke 1819–23

Crosses the Kupfergraben, Unter den Linden/Karl-Liebknecht-Strasse, Mitte

Karl Friedrich Schinkel

The only connection between the Crown Prince's Palace (now Humboldt University **21**) and the Stadtschloss (now destroyed) was the narrow wooden Hundebrücke (Dog Bridge) of 1806. With the increase in building work - Neue Wache **16** and alterations to the cathedral - a new bridge over the Kupfergraben, a tributary of the Spree, became an essential part of Schinkel's plans for central Berlin. Extending the line of the 'Linden', the bridge connects directly with the Lustgarten to the north of the

Stadtschloss which is subsequently upgraded to the principal town square.

In acknowledgement of the ceremonial route, Schinkel turned the bridge into a promenade lined by significant sculptures, perhaps influenced by the Charles Bridge in Prague which he had visited in 1811. Although opened in 1823, the eight groups of sculptures on the theme of war and peace were not completed until 1853–57 by various sculptors including Ludwig Wichmann and Friedrich Drake.

15 Zeughaus (Arsenal) 1695–1706

Unter den Linden 2, Mitte

Johann Arnold Nering, Martin Grünberg,
Andreas Schlüter

Commissioned by Friedrich I, the building work started in 1695 by Nering was completed after his death by Grünberg and Schlüter. The interiors, however, were not completed until 1730. The Royal Architect, Schlüter, while also being involved in the modelling of the nearby Stadtschloss, brought much of his artistry to the design. A Rome scholar, he was also an accomplished sculptor and along, with the figures on the façade, produced the twenty-two masks of dying warriors which adorn the inner courtyard. Allegorical figures of war appear in the tympanum with a bronze relief of Friedrich I above the main entrance. Regarded by many to be the most beautiful example of Baroque in Berlin, the square plan enables two well-balanced façades to address the Linden to the south and the Kupfergraben to the east. In 1880 work was completed in changing the building to a military museum by Friedrich Hitzig and the Second World War damage was repaired under the supervision of Otto Haesler. The building now serves as the museum for German history.

Zeughaus

Kronprinzenpalais

☞ Directly across the Linden at number 3 is the **Kronprinzenpalais** (1732) by Philipp Gerlach with additions in 1856 by Johann Heinrich Strack.

16 Neue Wache (New Guardhouse) 1816–18

Unter den Linden 4, Mitte

Karl Friedrich Schinkel

The Neue Wache replaced the old guardhouse, adjacent to the Zeughaus 15 which had been promoted to royal guardhouse in 1797, when Friedrich Wilhelm III, on ascending the throne, continued to live in the Kronprinzenpalais opposite. This, the first of Schinkel's three great masterpieces, was undertaken shortly after his promotion to Oberbaurat (Senior Adviser) under service to the king.

The building takes the form of a Roman castrum fronted by a Greek Doric temple portico. A guard

Old town centre and northern Friedrichstadt

room and various ancillary offices on two storeys led off an inner courtyard which was altered in 1931 by Heinrich Tessenow into a covered war memorial with an open skylight. The red brick used on the back and sides expressed the two storeys and highlights, by contrast, the monumentality of the granite frontage. The design displays characteristics which can be attributed to much of Schinkel's later works: overall certainty of proportion; consistency of surface and spatial relationships; and the fully reasoned significance of the details.

The ten sculptured figures along the entablature by Gottfried Schadow were complemented in 1846 by representations of Flight and Defeat, Struggle and Victory in the tympanum by August Kiss. This, together with the flanking statues to Field Marshals Scharnhorst and Bülow, would seem to support the interpretation that the building was also seen as a monument to the Wars of Liberation. In 1969 the Communist regime redesignated the building as a Memorial to the Victims of Fascism and Militarism.

17 Friedrichswerdersche Kirche (Friedrichswerder Church) 1824–30

Werderscher Markt, Mitte

Karl Friedrich Schinkel

The suburb of Friedrichswerder was the first expansion of the twin towns Berlin-Cölln and dates from 1662. Lying to the west and south of the old towns, it was included within the fortifications of 1685 and linked to the island of Cölln by the Gertraudenbrücke over the Kupfergraben. By the end of the eighteenth century, the original church of 1700 on the Werderscher Markt had fallen into disrepair and a decision was taken to replace it with a new building. Schinkel prepared four designs: two neo-Classical and two neo-Gothic. Crown Prince Friedrich Wilhelm chose the Gothic as the basis of a medieval style being more in keeping with a small site and the character of the surrounding quarter.

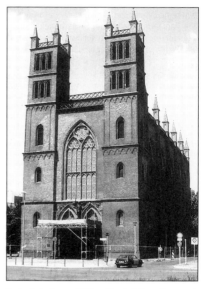

Schinkel never lost his fascination for Gothic and the exterior owes much to the English collegiate architecture he observed on his travels. A composition of simple forms and delicate proportions where two vertical flat roofed towers anchor a central horizontal flat-roofed nave. The horizontal articulation of the towers is balanced by the vertical expression of the side buttresses which terminate in pointed pinnacles. The single nave interior with its star vaulting displays more of the German tradition and Schinkel's inventiveness. Compound piers supporting the vaulting delineate the colonnaded side aisles and support an upper gallery which passes between the piers and the buttresses of the exterior wall. As Schinkel's first exclusively brick building, he demonstrates a great understanding for the material and

its technical possibilities. The building at present houses a collection of Schinkel's drawings, models and sculptures.

The church, together with its neighbour, the Bauakademie (Building Academy) of 1831–36 (demolished in 1961) extended the tradition of Berlin brick building and influenced many to follow. As part of the new urban design proposals for Schlossplatz, the Berlin Senat have decided to rebuild Schinkel's Bauakademie and Kommandantenhaus following the demolition of the GDR's Ausenministerium (Foreign Ministry) which was built on the site in 1964–67.

18 St Hedwigskathedrale (St Hedwig's Cathedral) 1747–73 rebuilt 1952–63

Bebelplatz, Mitte

Jean Laurent Legeay, Johann Boumann, Georg Wenzeslaus von Knobelsdorff

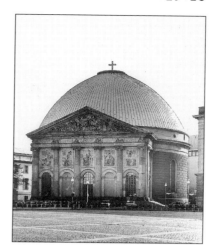

In 1740 when Friedrich II (Frederick the Great) came to the throne, work started on the Forum Fridericianum. The king's interest in architecture resulted in a collaboration with Legeay and Knobelsdorff to produce a church worthy of the new cultural centre of Berlin. The Frenchman Legeay, a friend of Piranesi, had studied in Rome, where he produced detailed survey drawings of the Pantheon. Knobelsdorff was principal architect for the design and following his death in 1753, the building was completed by Boumann the Elder and served as the church for the Catholic community. The building sits at an angle to the forum (now called Bebelplatz) relating originally to the star-shaped fortifications which were later demolished. Although elegant in their own way, the elliptical dome and circular plan seem to sit uneasily with the Roman portico. The reconstruction from 1952–63 was supervised by Hans Schwippert.

19 Staatsoper (German State Opera House) 1741–43

Unter den Linden 7, Mitte

Georg Wenzeslaus von Knobelsdorff

Friedrich II (Frederick the Great) was both a composer and performer of music and commissioned his 'Temple of Apollo' on a site adjacent to the then Royal Palace. This was the first major building to provide spatial definition to Friedrich's Forum and, together with St Hedwigs Cathedral, occupied the eastern edge. By comparison with von Knobelsdorff's next commission for Friedrich, the Rococo Sanssouci Palace (1745–47) **177**, the Opera House is more constrained and classical. The elongated cruciform plan with pedimented porticos projecting on all four sides is derivative of Palladio's Villa Rotunda. Internally there were three major spaces: the Apollo Room, the theatre stalls and the Corinthian Hall as a stage area. The build-

ing could also be used as a ballroom by means of raising the stalls with winches. The sculptural decoration, on the theme of Apollo and the Muses, was created by Johann August Nahl, Friedrich Christian Glume and Benjamin Griese. Following serious fire damage in 1843 it was rebuilt by Carl Ferdinand Langhans and again following the war damage of 1945 by Richard Paulick and Kurt Hemmerling.

☞ At Unter den Linden 5 is the **Prinzessinnenpalais** (now Operncafé) of 1733, by Friedrich Wilhelm Dietrichs.

Old town centre and northern Friedrichstadt

20 Alte Bibliothek (Old Library) 1775–80
Bebelplatz, Mitte
Georg Christian Unger

Following von Knobelsdorff's death in 1753, Unger became a favourite royal architect responsible for several palatial buildings in Potsdam. The Royal Library was the last building in Friedrich II's 'Forum Fridericianum' completed towards the end of his reign and demonstrates a stylistic move away from the neo-Classicism of the Opera House **19** and St Hedwigs Cathedral **18**. Unger was instructed to base the design on the Baroque Michaeler-Wing of the Hofburg Palace in Vienna which, due to various delays, was not completed until 1793. The Baroque curves of the façade with its large central portico and dominant end pavilions led to the nickname 'Commode'. From 1914 the building, together with the adjoining **Altes Palais** (1834–37) by Carl Ferdinand Langhans, has been part of the University.

21 Humboldt Universität 1748–53
Unter den Linden 6, Mitte
Johann Boumann

Originally built as a town palace for King Friedrich II's brother, Prince Heinrich, this building defined the northern end of the Forum Fridericianum. The work was executed by Boumann following designs by von Knobelsdorff with the side blocks not completed until 1766. Wilhelm von Humboldt (1767–1835) studied law and travelled extensively throughout Europe following his interests in language and aesthetics. While working in the Prussian Ministry of the Interior and holding the post as Head of the Education Department he founded the Friedrich Wilhelm University in Berlin in 1810.

The University originally occupied only part of the building with the expansion over the years leading to a large extension to the north in 1913–20 by Ludwig Hoffmann following the same style. The sculptural decoration was the work of Johann Peter Benckert, Johann Gottlieb Heymüller and Johann August Nahl. The marble statues of Wilhelm and his brother Alexander von Humboldt, by sculptors Reinhold Begas and Otto Paul were erected on either side of the entrance portal in 1883.

☞ Opposite the university, in the centre of Unter den Linden, stands the equestrian statue of Friedrich II (1840–51) by Christian Daniel Rauch.

22 Schauspielhaus (Concert Hall) 1818–21
Gendarmenmarkt , Mitte
Karl Friedrich Schinkel

The Gendarmenmarkt (the former Platz der Akademie) was the main public square in the Friedrichstadt expansion of 1740 covering three city blocks of the gridiron plan. Each block was developed to contain a monumental building, the French and German churches symmetrically placed on either side of the National Theatre completed in 1801. Schinkel became involved in designing stage settings for the theatre including twenty-six scenes for Mozart's opera *Die Zauberflöte* (*The Magic Flute*) which opened in Berlin in 1816.

When this original theatre by Carl Gotthard Langhans burned down in 1817, the king awarded Schinkel the commission to design the replacement.

Utilising the foundations and some remaining walls, Schinkel's design follows the north-south axis of the old building but dramatically counters this with the east-west orientation of the taller, central auditorium. Unity is achieved by applying a grid system of uniform pilasters over each of the building's façades. The pattern, expressing post and lintol, is derived from the Choragic Monument of Thrasyllus in Athens, a recurring theme in Schinkel's *oeuvre*. The overall composition of intersecting cuboid forms representing Greek edifices is lifted above the surrounding square on a giant podium. This provides the storage for scenery and increases the apparent scale of the entrance portico which incorporates the six Ionic columns from the previous building. The grand staircase afforded entrance to the bourgeoisie on foot crossing over the *porte-cochère* with the nobility arriving in their carriages below. The two wings accommodate a small concert hall and various rehearsal rooms.

The pictorial and sculptural ornamentation was largely designed by Schinkel himself and represents the myths of Apollo and Bacchus. Following extensive damage during the Second World War, the building has been restored with extensive internal alterations to create a larger concert hall and chamber music hall.

23 Französische Kirche (French Church)
1701; 1780

Gendarmenmarkt, Mitte

Louis Gayard, Karl von Gontard

Deutsche Kirche (German Church) 1701; 1780

Martin Grünberg, Karl von Gontard

The French Church by Louis Gayard was build in 1701 for the Huguenot refugees who had settled in Friedrichstadt. At the same time the German Church by Martin Grünberg was built on the other side of the Gendarmenmarkt to the south. When Friedrich II had the square redesigned in 1780, both buildings were extended by adding large domed structures which mirror each other across the square, based on the model of the Piazza del Popolo in Rome. They form a perfect symmetry which enhances the importance of the National Theatre by Langhans built later in 1801.

The buildings by Gontard with the lower sections based on Palladio's Villa Rotunda, are the last major works of Baroque Classicism. The sculptural decoration was designed by Daniel Chodowiecki. The French Church was rebuilt from 1978–83, with the Huguenot museum dating from 1926 reopening at the same time. The domed bell tower is accessed by a narrow winding stair which most surprisingly leads to a large restaurant in the roof spaces of the lower section.

The German Church is presently undergoing major renovation work.

Old town centre and northern Friedrichstadt

24 Commercial Building and Department Store *Galeries Lafayette* 1995

Friedrichstrasse, Mitte

Jean Nouvel

Part of the 'Friedrichstadtpassagen' development of three blocks linked underground by shopping arcades, this building contains both offices and a department store. Heights of the new buildings are based on the Berlin Building Regulations of 1929 which set an eaves height of 22 metres and a maximum ridge height of 30 metres which allowed for receding storeys at an angle of 60 degrees. Nouvel exploits this by adopting an angular geometry to the top of the block with subtle undulations relating to the internal inverted 'light cones' and the large central conical atrium. The glazing above the main entrance contains a 'serigraph', silver silk-screened print on the outside and a white one on the inside for projecting colourful images.

Between 1919 and 1921, Mies van der Rohe designed two glass-walled skyscraper office blocks for Friedrichstrasse, one prismatic and faceted, the other undulating and curvaceous, both inspired by Paul Scheerbart's *Glasarchitektur* of 1914. In his writing, Mies emphasises the importance of the reflective qualities of glass architecture more than the effect of light and shadow as in other buildings. During these early years, the simplicity of a 'skin and bones' approach also provided the building with a clarity and transparency. Seventy years later, the glass curtain wall has certainly become more sophisticated: multi-layered and fritted yet unfortunately more dense and impenetrable.

25 Brandenburger Tor (Brandenburg Gate) 1789–91

Pariser Platz, Mitte

Carl Gotthard Langhans

This enduring symbol of Berlin has borne witness to a turbulent period of history over the last two centuries. Friedrich Wilhelm I (the Soldier King) established the 'Linie' around the city in 1736, primarily as a customs wall, 14 kilometres long with fourteen gates. When built, the Brandenburg Gate terminated the 'Linden', the main east/west palace axis, at the wall and celebrated its continuation westward into the Tiergarten and on to the Charlottenburg Schloss **118**.

A work of Romantic Classicism, Langhans' design reflected the fashion for Greco-Roman architecture following the excavations of Pompeii in 1750. It is modelled on the Propylaeum on the Acropolis in Athens, with the entablature decorated in motifs inspired by those on the Parthenon. The bronze quadriga with Eirene, the victory goddess, bringer of peace, was not completed until 1793, to designs by Gottfried Schadow.

Ironically, Napoleon entered through the gate to occupy the city after defeating the Prussian armies in 1806 and had the quadriga removed to Paris. After the fall of Napoleon it was re-installed and Schinkel surmounted the staff which the goddess held with the Prussian eagle and a wreath of laurel leaves around the iron cross. During the Third Reich, the gate was frequently used as a backdrop for propaganda purposes, and by 1945 was badly mutilated and the quadriga destroyed.

After the war proposals were made by the Eastern authorities to adorn the gate with a model socialist family facing the rising sun. Fortunately, these were never realised and the war damage was repaired under Theodor Voissem in 1956 and a re-cast quadriga installed with the goddess' staff topped by an incongruous wreath. During the period of the Wall, the gate was isolated in the middle of no man's land accessible only by the military guards. Since unification the gate has been cleaned and the goddess restored to her pre-war glory. Now a tourist attraction, the gate plays host to the street sellers with their Communist memorabilia and fragments of the Wall.

26 Reichstag 1884–94, 1958–72, 1995–99 (proposed completion)

Platz der Republik 1, Tiergarten

Paul Wallot, Paul Baumgarten, Norman Foster

Ten years after the formation of the Second Reich, a competition took place for a building to house the Reichstag, or parliament. The winning design, by Paul Wallot, was completed in 1894. Built in the neo-Renaissance style much favoured during this period, the heavy bombastic characteristics are similar to those of other major buildings such as the Dom **9**.

In the 1920s an extension to the building was planned, but a new competition failed to produce a suitable solution. On 30 January 1933, the leader of the National Socialist Party, Adolf Hitler, was pronounced Chancellor by the President, von Hindenburg. During the night of 27 February the Reichstag burned, destroying the glass dome and the plenary chamber and marking the end of parliamentary democracy in Germany. After further damage in the Second World War, renovation work took place from 1958 to 1972, including internal additions by Paul Baumgarten in 1961, enabling the building to house an exhibition on German history.

Now that Berlin will once again be the seat of government, the Reichstag will be restored as the parliament building. An international competition resulted in the work being awarded to the English architect, Norman Foster. Paul Baumgarten's mezzanine floors will be removed with the original walls and arches restored to expose the spaciousness of the original interior. Restoration of the glazed dome will house a visitors' platform and provide natural light and ventilation. The advisory committee decided that the dome be round and the plenary chamber elliptical, symbolic of democracy and self-determination. The Bonn Government is committed to move to Berlin in 1998–2000 and the building is due to open in 1999.

Kaiser Wilhelm Gedächtniskirche (Kaiser Wilhelm Memorial Church) 27

New western centre and Tiergarten

**27 Kaiser Wilhelm Gedächtniskirche
(Kaiser Wilhelm Memorial Church)**
1961–63 (illustration opposite)
Breitscheidplatz, Charlottenburg
Franz Schwechten, Egon Eiermann

Both symbol and focal point to the new west, Eiermann's new church incorporates the remaining towers of the Kaiser Wilhelm Memorial Church of 1895 by Franz Schwechten. The original was built in a grand scale with six towers and lavish decoration, befitting Germany's first Emperor. A post-war debate regarding rebuilding or demolition resulted in an odd compromise with part of the remains, known as the 'Decayed Tooth',

being retained to incorporate a small museum. At the time this was both controversial and contrary to the general tendency of sweeping away prominent reminders of the war. By assembling new prismatic elements surrounding the old, Eiermann creates a varied composition juxtaposing old and new. A steel frame supports concrete panels perforated with stained glass, inspired perhaps by Auguste Perret's use of precast concrete elements at his church, Notre-Dame du Raincy (1924) outside Paris. The design here, however, is more severe and coldly mathematical. An electric blue glow emanates from the square grid of stained glass at night and during the day provides a suitable atmosphere for quiet reflection.

28 Europa Centre 1963–65

Tauentzienstrasse 9, Charlottenburg
Helmut Hentrich, Hubert Petschnigg

One of the most important planning projects of the 1960s in providing a new commercial focus to the new west, the complex occupies a key city block between Tauentzienstrasse and Budapester Strasse adjacent to the Kaiser Wilhelm Memorial Church **27** on Breitscheidplatz. Several important roads converge on this place with the 22 storey high-rise office block, with its revolving Mercedes roundel provides the pivotal marker for the site. The low level complex originally contained over one hundred shops, an exhibition space, two cinemas, twelve restaurants, a skating rink, several bars and cafés. Alterations during the 1970s and 1980s to cover in courtyards and passages have resulted in a somewhat disappointing and anonymous place, with atria and internal shops. The polished granite and cascading water of the globe fountain by Schmettau at the Breitscheid Platz entrance is a favourite meeting place, known as the 'wet dumpling'.

Globe fountain, Breitscheid Platz

New western centre and Tiergarten

29 **Kaufhaus des Westens (KaDeWe)** 1906–07

Tauentzienstrasse 21–24, Schöneberg

Johann Emil Schaudt

The decision by the Jandorf Company to build a new department store to the west of the city centre in 1906 has indeed proved prophetic. The contrast in appearance to other stores of the period was probably due to the polite residential nature of the district at the time. The Wertheim department store (1896) by Alfred Messel and the Tietz department store (1900) by Bernhard Sehring (both destroyed) combined historical sculpted ornamentation with large areas of glass on more innovative façades. Much of the original character with its small windows and restrained modelling survives despite additions in 1930, rebuilding in 1950 and the roof additions of 1993. With nearly 45,000 square metres of sales space, KaDeWe is one of Europe's largest stores. The interior appears somewhat dense and cramped lacking the usual orientation devices of a central atria or large stairwell. The gourmet department on the sixth floor is well worth a visit for its variety of eating outlets offering a large selection of local and international culinary delights. In addition to this the rooftop restaurant of the seventh floor provides good views of the city.

30 **U-Bahnhof Wittenbergplatz** 1911–13

Wittenbergplatz, Schöneberg

Alfred Grenander

The intersection of three lines in 1913 under Wittenbergplatz presented an opportunity to build a station in the middle of the square contrasting with the more inconspicuous siting of most other underground stations. The building provides a focal point to the square and marks the eastern edge of this commercial centre. Grenander's design harks back to the 1800s, Schinkelesque in its classical clarity with the cruciform plan appropriate for its pivotal position. The appearance of stripped Classicism is partly a result of a 1950s renovation which removed much of the war-damaged decoration. The interior of the central space has been partly restored to its pre-war splendour with decorative tilework and frescos.

31 **Grundkreditbank Centre** 1984–85

Budapester Strasse 35, Tiergarten

Hans Joachim Pysall, Peter Otto Stahrenberg

Corners are a vital element of city blocks. Historic Berlin enjoyed a great variety - pointed, rounded or chamfered - with or without conical or domed 'hats'. During the 1950s and 1960s, a preoccupation with free-standing blocks often resulted in open corners of negative space. The architects for the Grundkreditbank building used a bold curve on the acute angle between Budapester Strasse and Kurfürstenstrasse which provides several visual conflicts. The volume of the accommodation results in a massing which sits unhappily between the verticality of a tower and the horizontality of a curved façade. 'Traditional' red sandstone on a slender 'modern' frame combine with gold anodised aluminium curtain walling to create a confusion of vertical and horizontal elements on a building not quite sure what it wants to be. Then again, no one turns a corner quite like Mendelsohn!

32 Zoologischer Garten 1841–44
Hardenbergplatz, Tiergarten
Peter Joseph Lenné

The zoo gardens were founded in 1841 by a shareholding company outside the city gates on the southern bank of the Landwehrkanal, opening to the public in 1844. The zoo was stocked with a collection of 850 animals presented by Friedrich Wilhelm III from his private collection on the Pfaueninsel (Peacock Island) **155**. Lenné, who was involved with landscaping the Pfaueninsel and adjacent Tiergarten, designed the original layout which by the end of the nineteenth century had acquired an amusement hall, featuring regular concerts by a military band. The various enclosures and cages took on the theme of the animals' country of origin, but since the devastation of the war, many of the new buildings have a more neutral style. The Elephant Gate was reconstructed in the 1980s on its original site.

33 Bahnhof Zoologischer Garten 1934–40
Hardenbergstrasse 30, Charlottenburg
Fritz Hane

With the established growth expansion of this area beside the Zoo **32** and the Gedächtniskirche **27** during the 1930s came cafés, restaurants, theatres and galleries, creating a new centre. The new station was built with two halls: the lower for the electric S-Bahn trains and the upper for the smoky steam trains. Since the war, the station has become an important central interchange and terminus for the 'new west' and, granted the status of an 'ancient monument', was thoroughly renovated in 1984. A direct engineering approach using the 'popular' elements of steel portals and glass gives the building a timeless quality, entirely appropriate to its purpose.

☞ The recent kiosks and canopies on Hardenbergplatz for the underground and buses appear to be a Post-Modern homage to the U-Bahnhof Wittenbergplatz **30**.

34 Theater des Westens 1895–96
Kantstrasse 12, Charlottenburg
Bernhard Sehring

During the era of the Kaiserreich the westward development of new urban districts for the middle and upper bourgeoisie also included the construction of places of entertainment. This period of Prussian imperialism is reflected in the style of the front block with its ornate neo-Classical embellishments. Surprisingly, the complete building contains an odd combination of historical styles: French Renaissance façade with mock-medieval behind. Unfortunately, it is the medieval roofscape and flytower which is most prominent from the adjacent S-Bahn, presenting passengers to a feast of Disney/Brothers Grimm as the trains slow for the Zoo-Bahnhof.

Another building by Sehring - the celebrated Tietz department store of 1900 - was unfortunately destroyed during the Second World War. Its façade combined neo-Rococo iconography and sculpture with huge four-storey high shop windows which predated the modern curtain wall.

New western centre and Tiergarten

35 Kant Dreieck Media Centre 1994
Fasanenstrasse 81, Charlottenburg
Josef Kleihues

The competition brief called for a slender tower to provide a striking landmark on the site. In the winning design, the eleven-storey tower takes the form of a steel cube on top of a stone cube alongside a lower five-storey section which relates in scale to the neighbouring buildings. The lower section, triangular in plan, has a curved façade on its long side generated by the line of the adjacent 'S' Bahn. This 'shark's fin' shape is repeated on the enormous aluminium weathervane which sits on top of the tower and turns in the wind like a giant sail. This zoomorphic symbol, described by Kleihues as the building's 'cockscomb', undoubtedly provides a special identity and contributes to the desire for creating a new 'landmark'. A strong contrast is provided between the white metal cladding, with its exposed cross-bracing, and the grey granite cladding of the two cubes unified only by the pattern of square windows. Such whimsical idiosyncrasies are seen by the architect as a response to the area's tradition for artists, writers and theatre. The small public square alongside the building is planned to relate to the forecourt of Theater des Westens **34** across Kantstrasse.

36 Office Building 1994
Kurfürstendamm 70, Adenauerplatz, Charlottenburg
Helmut Jahn

Adenauerplatz, on the northern side of Kurfürstendamm, was bounded by the blank gable of a building which had survived the Second World War damage of its neighbours. During the 1970s, the creation of an inner-city expressway, Lewishamstrasse, cut across the Kurfürstendamm and had a detrimental effect on the scale and character of the area. The new building, therefore, is intended to cover the blank gable and serve as a landmark in the urban landscape. To overcome the narrowness of a site 20 metres wide but only 2.9 metres deep, the upper storeys cantilever out over the pavement to create more space: only the entrance hall, staircase and elevator occupy the ground plan. Drama is created on the corner by cantilevering the upper section of flat façade out from the curved pointed edge. Above the translucent façade of silver aluminium and fritted glass, the electronic advertising board and the 50 metre high 'antenna' add to the heroic constructivist image.

37 Schaubühne Theatre (formerly *Universum* Cinema) 1927–28, rebuilt 1978–81
Kurfürstendamm 153, Wilmersdorf
Erich Mendesohn, Jürgen Sawade

The Woga complex consisting of cinema, theatre, restaurant and residential demonstrates Mendelsohn's considerable abilities when working at the scale of urban design. This is somewhat at odds with the image of the architect's work conveyed by his series of beautiful broadline sketches always portraying the building as an object in isolation. Mendelsohn believed the cinema to be an exciting new building type, radically different from a theatre. The frontage consists of a dynamic composition of forms, hovering and revolving, pinned down by the advertisement tower. Sweeping curves are animated by dark bands of clinker brick and ribbon windows. The interior, with its double height foyer and elongated horseshoe plan, was rebuilt by Sawade as a convertible theatre auditorium. The adjacent block contains the original theatre behind the curved façade of the restaurant. The apartment buildings to the rear are also noteworthy with their semi-cylindrical stair towers to one side and rhythmical, flowing curved brick balconies to the other.

38 Deutsche Oper (German Opera) 1957–61
Bismarckstrasse 34–37, Charlottenburg
Fritz Bornemann

With the rebuilding of the Opera House, following the wartime destruction of the 1912 building by Heinrich Seeling, Bornemann adopted a brave new style. Requirements for a large amount of ancillary accommodation, including rehearsal spaces and workshops, on the small site were met by placing the auditorium hard against the building line on Bismarkstrasse. This main façade is a bold uncompromising plane of brushed concrete panels which serves as a neutral backdrop to Hans Uhlmann's balancing steel sculpture and creates a static street theatre. The simple cuboid form of the main auditorium hovers above the ground with the full height foyer windows facing the side street to one side and a small square to the other. This austere approach is carried into the auditorium with its democratic attempt to avoid any hierarchy amongst the audience.

A stylistic parallel in the 'East' can be found on Karl-Marx-Allee with the **Cinema International**, 1960–67 by Josef Kaiser.

New western centre and Tiergarten

39 Schiller Theater 1950–51

Bismarckstrasse 110, Charlottenburg

Völker & Grosse

The present building replaces the prestigious building of 1906 by Max Littmann which enjoyed great success during the heyday of popular theatre until its destruction during the war. Using simple geometric forms and good materials, it addresses a small square off Bismarckstrasse, the large curved form of the foyer window breaking through the smooth travertine wall with symmetrical formality. The visual problem of the flytower is handled subtly and effectively by the addition of a regular pattern of fluting. Conveying a certain 'Festival of Britain' aesthetic' the design stands the test of time with its careful proportions and refined details.

40 Technische Universität (Technical University) 1878–84, 1961–68

Strasse des 17. Juni 135, Charlottenburg

Richard Lucae, Friedrich Hitzig, Julius Carl Raschdorff;
Kurt Dübbers, Karl Heinz Schwennicke

Architecture Institute

The Technische Hochschule was established in 1879 by an amalgamation of the Bauakademie (Building Academy) and the Gewerbeakademie (Vocational Academy) moving to a new site west of the Tiergarten. The university commenced a considerable expansion in the 1950s and 1960s and now consists of a strange mixture of modern functionalism and historic fragments, often coming together on the same block. Of the original building by Lucae, Hitzig and Raschdorff completed in 1884, only the rear façade survived the war. The renovation and reconstruction by Dübbers and Schwennicke provides a stark contrast with a modernist expression for the new frontage.

☞ The **Architecture Institute** on Ernst-Reuter-Platz and Marchstrasse is housed in buildings by Bernhard Hermkes (1963–68) and Hans Scharoun with Bernhard Hermkes (1967–69).

41 Concerthall 1953–55

Hardenbergstrasse 32/Fasanenstrasse, Charlottenburg

Paul Baumgarten

The concert hall, stylistically similar to the Deutsche Oper **38** by Bornemann, was built at the front of the war-damaged Musikhochschule of 1902. It forms a curious neighbour to the adjacent Beaux Arts Hochschule der Künste by Kayser and Grossheim of 1898–1902 (illustrated below). This odd juxtaposition of old and new continues the pattern of the surrounding Technical University **40** and reflects the confidence of that age with its little concern for context. The intersection of two volumes is expressed by projecting the curved form of the hall roof above the rectangular two-storey block where a full height glass façade addressing the main street allows the expression of structural frame and reveals the human activity in the foyer behind.

Tiergarten

The name 'Tiergarten' meaning 'animal gardens' was given to the area of woodland and meadow south of the River Spree and to the west of the old town which became the Elector's hunting grounds from the sixteenth century onwards. As the city grew and its buildings gradually enveloped the park, the western edge was defined by the growth of Charlottenburg. Settlements were established in the northern area by the French refugees (Huguenots) during the early years of the eighteenth century, who cultivated the land and bred silkworms. In 1742 Friedrich the Great donated the royal hunting ground to the people of Berlin to use as a 'pleasure ground'. The royal architect, Georg Wenzeslaus von Knobelsdorff, was commissioned to introduce mazes, squares and the 'Venusbassin', today referred to as the 'Goldfish Pond'. It is this area, now the Grosser Tiergarten, which forms the basis of the present day park. Around 1800, country houses and summer residences for the rich appeared around the periphery followed by the cafés and beer gardens. The park was landscaped in 1833–39 by Peter Joseph Lenné, who drained the marches and constructed the canals. Lenné, a contemporary of Schinkel and director of gardens to Friedrich Wilhelm IV, overlaid a Baroque axial plan with a more English Romantic landscape. An area to the south-west, the former pheasantry, was laid out as a zoological garden **32**. From this period onwards, with Berlin as a capital and administrative centre, new embassies and consulates arrived to form a diplomatic quarter bordering the park to the south. After the Second World War, when Berliners were suffering from severe shortages, most of the trees were cut down for firewood and many of the lawns planted as vegetable gardens. Since 1949 much of the damage has been repaired and the park re-established as a recreational resource for the inner city.

42 Umlaufkanal (Waterflow Testing Station)
1975–76

Müller-Breslau-Strasse, Tiergarten

Ludwig Leo

The Versuchsanstalt für Wasserbau und Schiffsbau (Maritime Research Institute) has occupied this site on the Schleuseninsel since 1901. The institution originally tested models of ships for Kaiser Wilhelm II's fleet. The new building also serves the same purpose and the tubular water tank is considered the largest of its kind in the world. Leo turns the horizontal circulation channel on its side because of the narrow site expressing

this tubular element in pink and the measurement laboratories poised above it in blue cladding. This combination of technology and art results in a bizarre building with a strong sculptural identity.

New western centre and Tiergarten

43 Hansaviertel Interbau 1957 **(Permanent Housing Exhibition)** 1955–57

Klopstockstrasse, Bartningallee, Tiergarten

Oscar Niemeyer; Walter Gropius; Alvar Aalto; Arne Jacobsen; J. H. van den Broek, J. B. Bakema, et al.

The Hansa district on the north-western corner of the Tiergarten was one of the speculative residential developments resulting from the industrial expansion of the late nineteenth century. The middle classes inhabited the front buildings, with the poorer behind in the densely populated courtyards. It was the reaction against these often unsanitary conditions which led the modern architects of the 1920s and 1930s to create new environments 'at the heart of the metropolis in light, air and sun'. Following the severe damage of the Second World War, the Hansa area was chosen for the International Building Exhibition 'Interbau 1957', West Berlin's most important architectural event of the 1950s.

The urban planning and architectural aims were based on the ideals of the CIAM's Charter of Athens which primarily involved the zoning of the city with areas for residential use, work, cultural activities and recreation. Particular importance was placed on highways and fast traffic links to the different sections of the city. The aim to create a 'ribbon city', tailored to the needs of the motor car, negated the traditional concept of the European city along with the psychological suppression of history, particularly, of course, recent history. A total of fifty-four architects from thirteen countries, the elite of the day, contributed in a spirit of internationalism and open-mindedness.

The informal grouping of buildings includes two churches, a library, a kindergarten, a cinema and a small shopping centre. Five thousand people were accommodated in every type of residential building imaginable in the 1950s, ranging from the high-rise tower to the slab block to the low-rise terrace. Arne Jacobsen's small group of single-storey atrium houses offers a very different living opportunity to that of the two-level apartment in the sixteen-storey tower by van den Broek and Bakema. By contrast to Jacobsen's

1   *Berlin Pavilion*
2   *Walter Gropius*
3   *Wassili Luckhardt*
4   *Pierre Vago*
5   *Sergius Ruegenberg & Wolf von Mollendorf*
6   *Ludwig Lemmer*
7   *Paul Baumgarten*
8   *Arne Jacobsen*
9   *Alvar Aalto*
10 *Werner Duttman*
11 *Frotz Jaenecke & Sten Samuelson*
12 *Oscar Niemeyer*
13 *Egon Eiermann*
14 *Van den Broek & Bakema*

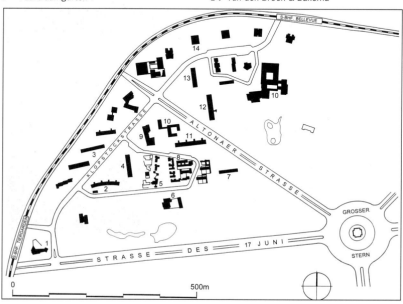

orthogonal approach, the cluster of single family houses by von Möllendorff and Ruegenberg conveys a much freer expressionism. White painted brickwork, timber panels and coloured steel 'Constructivist' elements stand out against the mature greenery of their surroundings. The slab block by Gropius relies on a pattern of projecting balconies with curved fronts like half-open drawers to characterise its otherwise bleak form. Niemeyer creates a more elegant block, like a miniature Corbusier Unité with a free standing sculptural stair tower. Alvar Aalto adapts the concept of the courtyard house for the apartment plans in his eight storey block. Corridors are eliminated by grouping ancillary rooms around a central living room and loggia which become the focus of family life. The subtle angling of the building and slight planar shifts of the façade at the loggias is enough to provide a rhythmic modelling to the otherwise sober functionalism.

Houses by von Möllendorff and Ruegenberg

Slab block by Walter Gropius

The Interbau's theme 'Living in the City of Tomorrow' encouraged an architecture of freedom and democratic rationalism. Working within the accepted ideology and considering the architects involved, the end results are largely disappointing. If you must live in a high-rise, however, this is not a bad place to be: an attractively landscaped parkland adjacent to the Tiergarten. Although the high-rise tower and slab block were also adopted by the authorities in East Berlin, they suffer by comparison because of their urban location and crude detailing. An exception to this strategy can be found in the monumental historicism of Strausbergerplatz 5 built at the same time in the East. It is interesting now to view both in comparison to the recent IBA initiatives which provide a 1980s vision of city planning using more traditional housing models.

Slab block by Oscar Niemeyer

☞ On the corner of Strasse des 17. Juni and Klopstockstrasse sits the **Berlin-Pavillon** built in 1956, by Fehling, Gogel and Pfankuch. Recently renovated for the Senatsverwaltung für Bau- und Wohnungswesen (Senate Construction and Housing Department), it is a popular venue for architectural exhibitions. Also as part of the 'Interbau 1957', Le Corbusier built a version of his Unité d'Habitation 139 near the Olympic Stadium 140 and the Congress Hall 45 to the east in the Tiergarten was designed by Hugh Stubbins.

Eight storey block by Alvar Aalto

New western centre and Tiergarten

44 Siegessäule (Victory Column) 1873
Grosser Stern, Tiergarten
Johann Heinrich Strack

In the centre of the Tiergarten Park, five roads converge at the Grosser Stern which functions now as a large traffic roundabout encompassing the Victory Column. Commissioned by Kaiser Wilhelm I to commemorate the triumphant Prussian campaigns against Denmark (1864), Austria (1866) and France (1870–71), the shaft is decorated with the barrels of captured cannon. Originally sited in Königsplatz in front of the Reichstag **26**, the column was moved to its present position on the east-west axis in 1938 and placed on top of a 6.5 metre high drum. Rising to an overall height of 67 metres, a staircase leads up to a viewing platform around the feet of the gilded statue. The work of the sculptor Friedrich Drake, Winged Victory has recently been restored to her original glory with a kilo of gold leaf.

The guard houses on the edge of Grosser Stern below the Siegessäule, were built before the war by Albert Speer. These small scale Neo-Classical temples with their tetrastyle of square columns expressing a simple post and lintol, reveal Speer's awareness of the earlier works of German Romantic Classicism. They now serve as public toilets.

45 Kongresshalle (Congress Hall) 1956–57
John-Foster-Dulles-Allee 10, Tiergarten
Hugh A. Stubbins

Built for the Internationale Bauaustellung of 1957 by the Benjamin Franklin Foundation, the Congress Hall was intended as a symbol of German-American friendship and gifted to the city by the USA. The site next to the Spree on the northern edge of the Tiergarten east of the Hansaviertel allows the building to be placed on axis to the Reichstag. The square podium contains a foyer, a small hall, conference and exhibition rooms and a restaurant. The flying roof over the main hall which seats 1,250 gives the building its nickname of the 'Pregnant Oyster'. This twin arched form, achieved by the use of reinforced concrete curved beams and suspended structure, represented an architectural advancement for the 1950s. Unfortunately in 1980 part of the roof collapsed following corrosion of its steel members and due to its symbolic significance the structure was rebuilt for the 750th anniversary celebrations held in 1987. The building is now listed as an architectural monument and remains a memorial to the age of tail-finned Cadillacs. The modern sculpture in the foreground is by Henry Moore.

☞ The **Carillon** (Bell Tower) of 1987, designed by Dietrich Bangert, Bernd Jansen, Stefan Scholz and Axel Schultes. Given to the city in 1987 by Daimler Benz to mark the 750th anniversary celebrations, the musical bell tower continues an eighteenth century Carillon tradition. The tower is 42 metres high and contains sixty-eight melodic bells, the biggest of which weighs over 7 tonnes.

46 Sowjetisches Ehrenmal (Soviet War Memorial) 1945

Strasse des 17. Juni, Tiergarten

The Soviet War Memorial, erected by the Soviets in November 1945, takes the form of a semi-circular colonnade crowned with an 8 metre high bronze soldier. Fashioned out of marble from Hitler's nearby destroyed Chancellery, the memorial is flanked by two tanks which saw action during the battle for Berlin. Throughout the duration of the Cold War soldiers of the Red Army defiantly stood guard despite its position in the Western Sector just to the west of the Brandenburg Gate 25.

47 Japanische Botschaft (Japanese Embassy) 1938–42

Tiergartenstrasse 26–27, Tiergarten
Ludwig Moshamer

Albert Speer's planned north-south axis required the demolition of several embassy buildings and those countries were given generous plots in compensation. The former villa area between the Tiergarten and the Landwehr Canal was developed by the Nazis into the diplomatic quarter. The new buildings had to conform to a style suitable for Hitler's vision of Germania which invariably led to a hard sterile neo-Classicism. Moshamer's design was built under Speer's direction and any Schinkelesque qualities are lost to the large scale and preference for flat columns. The raised central section of the attic strip carries a gold relief of the sun and a Japanese garden was planted between the wings to the rear.

After being damaged during the Second World War and standing empty, the building was renovated and converted in 1986–88 by Kisho Kurokawa and Taiji Yamaguchi for use as a Japanese-German cultural centre.

48 Kulturforum (Cultural Forum)

Post-war plans for rebuilding the inner city more often than not resulted in clearing sites and leaving them empty. The politicians' indecision in the occupied and divided city can be understood in the context of their hopes to retain capital status and having to face an increasingly uncertain future.

One plan which was at least partly realised was for the 'Cultural Belt' along the banks of the Spree between Museumsinsel and Charlottenburg Palace 118. The 'Cultural Forum', near Potsdamer Platz 56, was considered to play a key role as a link between east and west. This idea developed from Hans Scharoun's 'Ribbon Plan' for Berlin and his Philharmonie 49 was seen as its new heart. The 'Cultural Forum' today consists of a collection of disparate objects which look like chess pieces on the checkerboard of space. The Philharmonie sits at the opposite end of the architectural spectrum from the New National Gallery 53 and the Matthäi Church 52 appears incongruously like an unexpected visitor from the past. Only the latest museums recently completed on the western edge of the 'Forum' are attempting to create public space by relating to their immediate landscaped forecourts. Perhaps the unbuilt 'Forum' project by Hans Hollein in 1984 would have helped create a stronger definition of 'place', as the design drawings suggest.

New western centre and Tiergarten

49 Philharmonie (Philharmonic Hall) 1956–63
Matthäikirchstrasse 1, Tiergarten
Hans Scharoun

On its completion in 1963, the Philharmonie set a new standard for world-class concert halls. The controversial exterior is of secondary importance to the main function of the hall, its organic expressionism defying the usual terms of reference. It is intriguing to compare it with Scharoun's early works of mainstream modernism up until 1933 when the Nazi 'Heimatstil' forced him into an interior exile of spatial experimentation. Perhaps this period marked a change in direction or a change in priorities. Originally, the shuttered concrete walls of the auditorium were painted yellow-ochre. Following the completion of the State Library **51**, they were clad with gold anodised aluminium profiled panels, a finish which is shared by the Chamber Hall **50** and the Library.

The impressive foyer provides a perfect foil to the hall, occupying the space below its curved underbelly supported by V-shaped columns. An extended system of stairways and galleries enables individuals to see and be seen on arrival and during the interval. Extraordinary light fittings and coloured glass lenses have a festive quality and heighten the sense of anticipation.

Scharoun described the interior of the hall as a 'landscape': the auditorium representing a valley with the orchestra at its bottom, surrounded by tiers of vineyards climbing the sides. The ceiling, resembling a tent, forms a 'skyscape'.

This modern abstraction of the old arena places the audience around the stage subdivided into terraces comparable in size with the orchestra and thereby reduces the usual contrast and separation between performers and listeners. A sense of community is given to each terrace by providing each with a separate entrance. Unlike the traditional arena, the angular variations of each terrace ensures that the focus is not only on the orchestra but also with other groups of the audience, thus heightening its self-awareness and increasing the sense of equal participation in a shared experience. The varying angles, tilting floor planes, and skyscape with acoustic 'clouds' defy conventional ideas of perspective and create a celestial atmosphere. The excellent acoustics are due to the input of Lothar Cremer who worked together with Herbert von Karajan, then Conductor-in-Chief, in achieving such a 'lively' acoustic. An evening with the Berlin Philharmonic Orchestra performing in Scharoun's spatial masterpiece remains one of life's magical experiences.

50 Kammermusiksaal (Chamber Music Hall)
1984–87

Matthäikirchstrasse 3, Tiergarten
Hans Scharoun, Edgar Wisniewski

The project for the Chamber Music Hall, part of Scharoun's original plan for the Cultural Forum, was finally realised over twenty years after the Philharmonie **49**. Constructed after Scharoun's death in 1972 by his associate, Edgar Wisniewski, the design follows a similar concept to its neighbour and predecessor. With a central stage surrounded by identifiable banks of seating, flexibility of layout is achieved by their interchangeability. A combination of steep terracing and grouping the audience into autonomous tiers results in a great number of people being close to the performance and achieves a feeling of greater intimacy associated with chamber music. The abstract visual language of the exterior is carried over from the Philharmonie. Although the design is inevitably associated with Scharoun, Wisniewski should be credited for overcoming the red tape and financial setbacks in realising the project.

51 Staatsbibliothek (State Library) 1967–78

Potsdamer Strasse 33, Tiergarten
Hans Scharoun, Edgar Wisniewski

In 1964, Scharoun was awarded First prize with this competition entry for the Prussian State Library. Unfortunately, he did not live to see its completion and the building works were completed by Wisniewski.

Defining the eastern edge of the Cultural Forum and separated from the other buildings by an urban motorway, the State Library occupies the site of the original Potsdamer Strasse. The public circulation of cascading and spiralling stairways ties together a collection of large and small spaces on different levels culminating in the large volume of the vast block at the rear with its distinctive silhouette. Externally the combination of these different elements appears over-complicated and confused, a building complex with the expression of an accretive design. The main 'hull' is clad in the same gold profiled panels as the Philharmonie **49** and the Chamber Music Hall **50**. Considered to be the largest library building in central Europe, its collection of manuscripts is one of the most comprehensive in the world.

New western centre and Tiergarten

52 Matthäikirche (Matthäi Church)
1844–46

Matthäikirchplatz, Tiergarten

Friedrich August Stüler

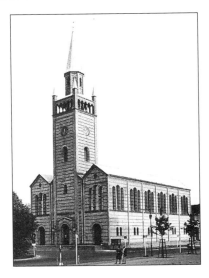

Surviving the Speer demolitions of 1938, the church was damaged by fire in 1945 and rebuilt between 1956 and 1960. The open nature of this new context is at odds with the axial symmetry of the hall church plan (the original context was more tightly contained and symmetrical). Stüler's work expresses the spirit of the age with its interest in early Italian architecture. The design combines elegant proportions with a controlled geometry which simply expresses the plan elements of a central nave, flanked by two subsidiary aisles with choir, two side apses and campanile. There is a rawness and fragility about the striped brickwork which makes its survival even more surprising.

53 Neue Nationalgalerie (New National Gallery) 1965–68

Potsdamer Strasse 50, Tiergarten

Ludwig Mies van der Rohe

When the Bauhaus was finally closed down in 1933, its last director, Mies van der Rohe, submitted an entry for the Reichsbank competition in Berlin. The unrealised design represented a move from informal asymmetry to symmetrical monumentality which later culminated in an idiom widely adopted by the American building industry and its corporate clientele in the 1950s. Mies reinterpreted the ancient elements of column, beam, roof and wall to create his 'universal space' with a skeletal steel frame. Glass walls change under different light conditions from a reflective surface to one of pure transparency.

The New National Gallery transfers much of the work developed with the IIT campus buildings in Chicago back to Berlin. This neo-Classical temple of steel and glass sits on a podium of granite with

familiar details from the formal vocabulary of the architects oeuvre. The glazed space under the deep coffered steel roof supported on eight columns is used only for temporary exhibitions because of difficulties in controlling natural light. The main gallery spaces, housing the permanent collections of ninteenth-and twentieth-century art, inhabit the subterranean podium and open on to the outdoor sculpture court. Success hovers between architectural honesty and emotional ambivalence where, on the Cultural Forum, the silence of Mies contrasts with the music of Scharoun.

54 Wissenschaftszentrum (Science Centre)
1984–88

Reichpietschufer 48–58, Tiergarden
James Stirling, Michael Wilford

This is the largest individual non-housing complex in the IBA programme and the most monumental. The design conforms to the 'urban landscape' concept of Scharoun for siting individual buildings in a Cultural Forum with its museums, libraries and concert halls. The design had to incorporate the renovated Reichsversicherungsamt (Imperial Insurance Office) of the German Reich, originally built in 1891–94 by August Busse, which is listed. This building, which addresses the Landwehr Canal, is one of the few from the era of the Kaiserreich which is still standing. Its heavily rusticated base and keystones with sculpted masques express the architectural concerns of the period. Clustering around the courtyard to the rear of the existing building are four new buildings, each representing a great historic archetype; church, stoa, campanile and amphitheatre. A fifth building, the castle, remains unbuilt due to financial cut-backs and is expressed as a footprint in the landscape. Three separate institutes were brought together on the site to share conference rooms, a library in the tower and central administration in the existing building. Expressing each institution by its own building is an attempt to avoid a single 'institutional' aesthetic with only the pattern of windows and striped colour scheme unifying the complex. Much of the detail design relies also upon historicist quotations: sugaricing colours which refer back to Berlin's Baroque and Rococo; hooded window surrounds from Ernst Sagebiel's Tempelhof Airport **112** and the Air Ministry Headquarters **81**; and primary coloured steel elements of Constructivism. To Berliners, the building has become known as the 'Wedding Cake'.

55 Shellhaus (Bewag Office Building) 1930–31
60–62 Reichpietschufer, Tiergarten
Emil Fahrenkamp

One of the first high-rise steel-framed constructions in the 'Neue Sachlichkeit' style, the Shellhaus rightly deserved its historical acclaim. Originally owned by the Shell Oil Company, it was taken over by the neighbouring Imperial Navy Office in 1940 and the Bewag (Berlin Gas and Electric) since 1946. Presently unoccupied, it now sits in a sad state of disrepair awaiting renovation. The accomplished design responds to the site context by placing the 'tower' on the main road corner and by stepping back and reducing height the façade offers a 'wave' frontage to the angular line of the canal, bringing down the scale to meet the neighbouring blocks. Horizontal layers of ribbon window and limestone spandrels serve to accentuate the curves reminiscent of the expressionism of Mendelsohn.

New western centre and Tiergarten

56 Potsdamer Platz
Started 1992, proposed completion 1998

For many years, the one surviving structure, part of an old apartment block, stood isolated like a ghost on the scorched patch of ground that was once one of Europe's busiest public spaces. Until the later days of the war, the square was the gateway to the inner city and the hub of its public transport system. Potsdamer Platz, together with the adjacent octagon of Leipziger Platz, was born out of the eighteenth century Baroque ground plan where the Potsdamer Gate was a point of intersection of long streets that cross the city and continue into the countryside. During the time of the Wall much of the space was held captive in no man's land as East and West developed new centres. Following unification, the 'Zentrale Bereich' has been rediscovered, its pivotal position forming a link between the old historic centre in the east the new commercial district in the west.

The strategic and political importance of the site has hindered the owners, Daimler- Benz, Sony and ABB in making headway with various competition-winning schemes which have raised controversies. The Munich architects, Hilmer and Sattlers were awarded first prize in the urban design competition held in 1991. The plan, which retains the historic radial street patterns creates 50 by 50 metre urban blocks with retail and service at street level and office and residential above.

The Sony complex includes a tower and contains a glass-roofed public forum designed by Helmut Jahn. The Daimler-Benz site, planned by Renzo Piano, includes individual buildings by Richard Rogers, Arata Isozaki, Giorgio Grassi and Hans Kollhoff.

The entire project, which includes nineteen separate buildings, is due for completion in 1998.

Internationale Bauausstellung (IBA)

The Internationale Bauausstellung (International Building Exhibition), or IBA for short, was started in 1979 to promote urban development on a human scale of high artistic quality set against the acknowledged deficiencies of post-war development in the city.

The motto 'inner city as a place to live' has gained new currency since many of the IBA areas are now in the middle of the united city and no longer on the edge of the western sector. The IBA had two principal concerns: 'Careful Urban Renewal' under the direction of Professor Hardt-Waltherr Hämer and 'Critical Reconstruction', directed by Professor Josef Paul Kleihues. The scale of the operation was enormous, involving input from the residents, the districts, and the city authorities right through to the international experts. Much of the work was completed by 1987 to coincide with the city's 750th birthday celebrations with the private successor organisation STERN (Gesellschaft der behutsen Stadterneurung Berlin mbH) then founded with the aim of continuing and extending the work started by IBA.

IBA areas are located at Tegel to the north-west and Prager Platz to the south of the western centre, with the biggest concentration of the old centre at southern Tiergarten, southern Friedrichstadt and Luisenstadt. These sections in the guide also include important non-IBA buildings where their geographic location falls within an IBA area.

IBA southern Tiergarten

The area of woodland and meadow south of the River Spree was used as the Elector's hunting ground from the sixteenth century onwards. In 1742 it was given to the people of Berlin to use as a 'pleasure ground' and by 1800 the rich were building country houses and summer residences on the periphery. In the mid nineteenth century, Peter Joseph Lenné was commissioned to lay out a landscaped park draining an area of marsh and creating the canal with its tree-lined boulevards.

With Berlin's new capital status from 1871, and the new station in Potsdamer Platz, the area's proximity to the seat of government and quality of urban life attracted embassies and consulates. This pattern continued up until the Second World War when are area suffered extensive destruction. Until the IBA began, there had been little new building except for the Kulturforum which is a controversial project, still incomplete.

The biggest number of IBA projects lie on the south side of the Landwehr Canal with only a limited number to the north side on the edge of the park. The main aims were to repair the urban fabric, close up gaps in the blocks, repair the edge of the park and create new urban green spaces. The state-subsidised housing also included designs which were to fit in with the traditional villa character. Playgrounds, day-care centres, schools and youth leisure facilities were also provided.

IBA southern Tiergarten

57 **Urban Villas in Rauchstrasse** 1983–84
Rauchstrasse 4–10, Thomas-Dehler-Strasse
38–47, Tiergarten

*Rob Krier (including the masterplan), Francy
Valentiny, Hubert Hermann; Hans Hollein;
Aldo Rossi; Henry Nielebock; Giorgio Grassi;
Klaus Theo Brenner, Benedict Tonon*

Rob Krier's gateway building

Villa by Hans Hollein

This important site, on the southern edge of the
Tiergarten, had one surviving building which
served as a reminder of the area's pre-war status.
The former Luxembourg Embassy (from 1938
the Norwegian Military Mission) became the cor-
nerstone for Rob Krier's IBA competition-winning
scheme of 1980. The ground plan consists of
two rows of five urban villas, incorporating the
existing former Embassy, enclosing a central
linear garden. Six of nine new villas take the form
of five-storey cubes, one echoes the rectangular
form of the embassy building and the other two
are linked by a curved section with an arched
entry to the garden. The urban villa can be seen
as a development of the nineteenth century suburban villas and mansion houses which, as a
result of changing economic circumstances, were
subdivided into several apartments without los-
ing their individual character, quiet living style,
and close contact to nature. Krier's strategy
involved six other architectural firms contributing
designs which give each villa its own identity and
ensures an interesting mix. With the open block
ground plan, the size of the villas and their
proximity becomes crucial in creating a sense of
enclosure for the internal space. The finished
scheme succeeds here by a simple use of trees,
pathways and raised and lowered grass planes.

Krier's gateway building uses a crescent-shaped
central section to close off the inner garden and
shield the space from the noise of Stülerstrasse.
The two end blocks relate in scale and form to the
free-standing cube villas and bring the different
elements of the group together. A path leads
through the archway in the centre of the façade
setting up an axial symmetry which further serves
to unite the group. A large aluminium bust deco-
rates the archway - a laughing figure with a
Venetian mast sculpted by Gero Schwanberg
from Vienna after a design by Krier. Red brick and
white painted stucco, the two finishes favoured in
the scheme, are both used on the gateway
building to good effect. The white curved surface
of the centre highlights the 'entrance', separates
the end blocks and dramatises the straight flights
of stairs on either side of the archway. Brickwork
predominates on the garden side where the
concave curve of the central section is framed by

two towers. With balanced asymmetry, Krier
describes the right-hand one as characterising
German 'severity', while the left-hand one has
Italian 'noblesse'.

The neighbouring villa on Rauchstrasse by
Hermann and Valentiny from Luxembourg is recognisable by the dazzling stripes of the ground
floor. The composition relies on the traditional
layering of strong base, central section and attic
storey. Terraces inserted on the east and west
sides break up the cube into a cluster of towers.
Colour is added to the predominantly white stucco
in a powerful way. Alternating stripes of yellow
and red wrap around the base with the yellow
carried up on either side of the main entrance
balconies.

The use of colour on the next villa by Hans Hollein
from Vienna is further used to reinforce the
various manipulations of the building's mass.
Hollein introduces 'breaks' in the cubic form with
projecting balconies, recessed stairwell and oriel
windows. Cuts in the large overhanging eaves
adds further drama to this differentiation between static cubic forms and dynamic interven-

tions. The traditional tripartite is expressed on the corners by a hierarchy of windows topped by an open loggia under the eaves. The curved projections of the oriel windows on adjacent planes are geometrically aligned to describe the insertion of a glazed drum into the solid corner. A red-brown colour gives weight to the base and contrasts with the extraordinary pink 'crazy paving' finish to the wall section beside the yellow stair tower.

The Swiss architect, Mario Botta, worked on the design of a villa for the scheme. Krier claims that following a dispute regarding the restrictive conditions for planning and construction he resigned his commission leaving him with a redesign. The resultant villa provides a sense of fun by producing variations on a theme for the façades and applying different visual ideas for the four corners. Elements such as column, lintol, ledge and balcony are brightly coloured, particularly on the south elevation. Unfortunately, this collage of Post-Modern imagery already looks very dated.

The red brick block by Aldo Rossi from Milan has a more enduring quality. The rectangular plan, with its subtractive corner, is respectful in scale and form to the neighbouring embassy block without being sentimental. Rossi uses the re-entrant corner to good advantage by carving into the block to reveal the stair tower with its octagonal lantern, a favourite element. Flanked by white painted stucco balcony recesses, the red brick tower continues a dialogue with the Krier entry block towers at the other end of the scheme. The success of Rossi's block owes much to considered proportions and careful detailing. The outer façades are given twin stripes of yellow brick tying together windows and loggia openings. A fine articulation to the regular openings is given by the green painted indented steel lintols which also provide the architect's signature.

The neighbouring villa on Thomas-Dehler-Strasse, by the Berlin architect, Nielebock adopts a symmetrical ordering on each façade. The corners are defined by reinforced concrete balcony frames in a similar way to Krier's end blocks. A four-storey cluster of balconies, or large windows, forms the central articulation of each façade leaving a repetitive pattern of smaller windows to denote the attic storey.

The next villa, by Giorgio Grassi from Milan, displays the harder qualities of austere Rationalism. The loggia recesses, from base to eaves, divide the cube into a group of towers. This

Corner block by Aldo Rossi

Villa by Henry Nielebock

regular distribution of windows and calm precision of detailing is reminiscent of the reductionism of the 1950s.

The Berlin architects, Brenner and Tonon, take much of their inspiration from the modern movements of the 1920s and 1930s. With a strict avoidance of symmetry and regular patterns of horizontal windows, this white villa shares some of its neighbour's hardness. A subtle relief is offered by the double-height entrance with its curved balcony and corner.

The scheme contains a total of 239 dwellings. The cubic villas contain twenty-four apartments, four on the ground and five on each of the upper floors. Although there is a mix of one, two and three bedrooms, the apartment sizes, finishing standard and building regulations were the same for all the buildings.

IBA southern Tiergarten

58 Four Linked Urban Villas 1981–82
Rauchstrasse 19–20, Tiergarten
Dietrich Bangert, Bernd Jansen, Stefan Scholz, Axel Schultes

Although not an IBA project, this group of four four-storey apartment blocks is one of the first examples of the 'urban villa' which was rediscovered in the Berlin Summer Academy of 1977, directed by Oswald Matthias Ungers. The design approach here is from the 'inside out' unlike the IBA's 'outside in' across Rauchstrasse. Each of the four corner blocks contains four maisonettes with double height windows and loggias. These 'raised gardens' form bridge links between the blocks to enclose the central space and frame the views out. The raised central court provides a sheltered intimate space and the architectural language of primary forms and simple finishes is pleasantly refreshing. Car parking is contained within a semi-basement and naturally vented through a circular cut-out in the centre of the court which encompasses a solitary tree.

59 Ökohaus (Ecology Housing) 1988–90
Rauchstrasse 21, Corneliusstrasse 11–12, Tiergarten
Frei Otto (concept), Hermann Kendel et al.

The Eco-house project for twenty-six residential units and one commercial unit resulted from an initial study by Frei Otto. The owners co-operated with Otto and other architects in designing a self-build scheme as an experiment in ecologically sound living. Careful consideration was given to maximising the use of the site while retaining existing trees and minimising environmental impact. Issues of energy efficiency and sustainability were addressed by incorporating solar devices, heat recovery, power saving measures and water recycling. Roofs and terraces are planted as compensation for ground lost to building and the construction used ecologically sound materials. Its appearance therefore reflects its ethos and material concerns.

60 Bauhausarchiv 1976–78
Klingelhöferstrásse 13–14, Tiergarten
Walter Gropius, Alexander Cvijanovic

The Bauhaus, born out of a continuous effort to reform applied art education in Germany, sought to remove the barriers between artist and craftsman by advocating a workshop-based education. Walter Gropius, having originally founded the Bauhaus in Weimar in 1919, designed new buildings for the school's relocation to Dessau in 1925. It was effectively closed down by the Nazis in 1933 following increasing pressure for its left-wing tendencies. What was left, under the directorship of Mies van der Rohe, moved to a warehouse on the outskirts of Berlin where nine months later it finally closed. In 1964, Gropius designed the archive for a site in Darmstadt to house the school's surviving material. After his death, it was decided to build in Berlin and Cvijanovic made only minor changes to the design. It would seem, however, that the long entrance ramp and ceremonial route over the building have lost some meaning in the move from a sloping to a flat site. The exhibition spaces are top-lit by the distinctive curved skylights which, crowded tightly together, give the building its unmistakable character.

61 Lützowplatz

The square was conceived in the Hobrecht plan of 1862 as the 'Gateway to the Tiergarten'. The north-south axis between Grosser Stern and Nollendorfplatz cuts diagonally across the square although the roads pass around the edge. Before it was damaged during the war its rectangular urban form was defined by residential blocks on three sides and the Landwehr Canal on the other. After the war, new plans ignored its previous character and created a large traffic intersection. IBA produced a development plan in 1983 to redesign the square by reinstating the buildings, narrowing the roads and landscaping the green area. An open competition held in 1986 resulted in five equal prizewinners whose proposals were revised and completed in 1991 by Wehberg, Müller and Knippschild. Residential blocks were built on the east and west sides and an extension to the Hotel Berlin on the south side. Completed in 1987, the hotel by Brenner and Tonon preserves a façade of strong horizontal bands to the square, sweeps around the corner to Einemstrasse, and creates a rhythm of window projections which look north back to the square on the Grosser Stern. The corner is reminiscent of some of Erich Mendelsohn's works lost to the war.

Lützowplatz

Hotel by Brenner and Tonon

IBA southern Tiergarten

62 Residential Complex 1982–84
Lützowplatz 2–16, Tiergarten
Oswald Matthias Ungers

Ungers' scheme reinstates the western edge of the square and completes the existing perimeter block. Although the design presents a continuous wall of building to Lützowplatz, due to traffic noise, it orientates itself inwards to a new environment. Behind this linear block is a row of three villas and two gateway blocks attached to the existing perimeter. This north-south pattern provides a public edge for the square to the east, a semi-private street within the block to the west and a private pedestrian route in between. The internal street leads to parking, both open and underground. Raised terraces and private gardens look on to the winding pedestrian path where children can safely play. The double pitched roofs of the villas are reflected in the Lützowplatz frontage which appears rather austere. Red brick terraces and plinths help to relieve the predominance of grey stucco which resulted from cost cuts. The original design drawings, although still following Ungers' strict rationalism, illustrate a use of more brickwork with timber pergolas for the pathway.

63 Residential Park beside Lützowplatz 1987–93
Lützowplatz 1–5, Lützowstrasse 57–66, Einemstrasse 18–26, Tiergarten
Bangert, Jansen, Scholz, Schultes;
Peter Cook, Christine Hawley
Mario Botta; Harald Deilmann;
Christian de Portzamparc; Seigfried Gergs;
AGP, Hans Heidenreich, Michael Polensky,
Reinhard Vogel, Helmut Zeumer;
Hans-Peter Störl; Bartels, Schmidt-Ott; Werner
Goehner; Heinz Hilmer, Christoph Sattler;
Max and Karl Dudler; Klaus Baesler,
Bernhard Schmidt, Ante Josip von Kostelac

This large IBA scheme consists of developments on the edge of the block and also in the interior. The perimeter buildings include shops and offices on Einemstrasse and residential apartments in Lützowplatz continuing around the corner to Lützowstrasse. The interior of the block includes a child day-care centre, nine urban villas, and private green areas. An internal network of routes allows access and leads to the Landwehr Canal and the Tiergarten beyond.

Apartments by Bangert, Jansen, Scholz and Schultes

The group of three new apartment blocks on the eastern edge of Lützoplatz extends the line of existing buildings and completed the north-eastern corner of the square. Bangert, Jansen, Scholz and Schultes use a brickwork frame of double height openings sitting above the café and shop on the ground floor. The glass curtain wall of each maisonette is recessed at 45° to form a triangular balcony with a semi-circular balcony project-

Apartments by Peter Cook and Christine Hawley

ing though the glass above. The façade displays a strong order and modelling by simple geometries.

The neighbouring building by Peter Cook is more whimsical. Angular openings and tilting planes combine with cascading glazed balcony projections and loose curves to create an anarchic façade. Turquoise metalwork provides the colour accent and much is made of the rainwater pipe. Cook, best known as a teacher and theorist, revels in the freeform of self-expressionism, happily ignoring the mathematical precision of the buildings on either side.

The corner block by Mario Botta is a combination of familiar moves from his existing body of work. Although the attention to detail is as high as one would expect, certain low cost finishes are an unfamiliar surprise. The stainless steel column cladding is in fact silver painted concrete and the black-white marble bands are painted bricks, highlighting perhaps the material differences between Lugano and Berlin. The 'open' corner uses a strong diagonal cut across the double height ground floor with recessed curved balconies above, exposing the planal quality of the reticulated brickwork façades.

Apartments by Mario Botta

The perimeter of the block is completed along Lützostrasse with eight buildings by six architects forming a coherent north-facing street frontage. Fenestration follows various anonymous patterns with the white stucco walls tied together by a red-brown brick ground floor base. The building by Christian de Portzamparc from Paris carries a stronger identity than the others. The symmetrical façade uses the traditional tripartite horizontally and vertically with a constructivist cylindrical stair tower in the centre.

Apartments by Christian de Portzamparc

The largest space in the interior of the block is used as a sports ground by the existing French lycée. This has been augmented by a new playground for the childs day-care centre by Baesler and Schmidt which occupies the northern part of the space. The visual impact of the building on the space is reduced by half sinking the one- and two-storey block into the ground. The 'U' shaped plan embraces a sunken playground which is thereby defined and protected from the open space. The interior landscape of the block is also delineated by two rows of urban villas, each by different architects. Adopting space standards set down by the 'Rationalisierungskatalog' (German public housing standards) resulted in a volume approximating a 12-metre cube. Most of the architects display a determination not to be dominated by

Day-care centre and urban villas

the 'cube' by expressing the internal ordering of spaces and dealing with the material aspects of the walls. As with so many of the IBA projects, clinker brick and stucco predominate. Although the designs by Hans-Peter Störl and Siegfried Gergs both adopt a nine-square plan, their volumetric expressions are diametrically opposed: one having a centralised cruciform in brick with stucco corners and the other having four brick towers with stucco infill.

In the south-west corner of the internal court are two commercial buildings which enfront Einemstrasse. Alongside its square-gridded, metal-clad neighbour, the office building by Hilmer and Sattler reveals a more subtle and refined approach to the art of

Commercial building by Hilmer and Sattler

street façades. Clad in small terracotta panels, the design involves a clever use of this traditional material, with its colour and texture, in a contemporary idiom.

64 Gatehouses in Lützowstrasse 1984–86

Lützowstrasse 43–51, Tiergarten

Vittorio Gregotti

The archetypal gateway building continues the definition of the street by retaining the integrity of the perimeter block while signalling public access to the space within. The design by Vittorio Gregotti of Milan, consisting of sixty-four apartments and four shops allows access to four rows of townhouses **65** and pathways through the block to the new footbridge over the Landwehr Canal. Two five-storey gatehouses are linked by a four-storey centre section in yellow brick with red banding. Dark metal clad-

ding is used on oriel windows and to emphasise the three-storey openings which contain corner shops at the base. Gregotti demonstrates his capabilities in balancing colour, contrast, projection and recess in an individualistic response to context.

65 Town Houses 1984

Lützowstrasse 46–51, Tiergarten

Brant, Heiss, Liepe, Steigelmann; Otto Steidle; von Gerkan, Marg; Oefelein und Freund; Manfred Schiedhelm

Protected from the street by the gatehouse apartment block **64**, thirty-six town houses in four rows offer their private owners a different living opportunity. The concept for the project, with its theme of living close to the city centre in a small versatile house, arose from a competition promoted by the Federal Minister for Regional Planning, Building and Urban Development. Each house contains an apartment and larger residence with hobby rooms, garden and garage. The small scale and narrow roads create a mews atmosphere and the owner-occupiers ensure a social mix with the adjacent state-subsidised apartments.

66 Footbridge Hiroshima-Steg formerly Lützowbrücke then Graf-Spree-Brücke, 1987

Crosses the Landwehr Canal, Lützowufer/
Reichpietschufer, Tiergarten

Klaus Theo Brenner, Benedict Tonon

As part of the IBA urban development plan, the original intention was to rebuild the bridge from plans and pictures of the original. This idea had to be revised owing to the increase in height required by shipping. Although Brenner and Tonon's design retains the salient features of the original, it differs in one major way. While the original walkway simply sat on the crossbeams of the top arch, the new solution allows the passage of the walkway to be suspended from the arch, using colour to differentiate the two elements. This complicated intermingling of structural elements apart, the details of the steelwork and masonry abutments are carefully considered and rigorously executed. The bridge is now the centrepiece of a network of pedestrian and cycle routes which link up the new housing complexes with the diplomatic quarter and the Tiergarten park.

67 Five Energy Saving Villas 1983–85

Lützowufer 1a–5a, Tiergarten

*Bernd Faskel, Vladimir Nikolic; von Gerkan,
Marg; Pysall, Jensen, Stahrenberg;
Kilpper; Manfred Schiedhelm, Karen Axelrad;
Hannelore Kossel (landscape)*

Villa by Scheidhelm and Axelrad

Increasing demands and rising costs of fuel during the 1970s led to many questions regarding energy efficiency in the 1980s. This scheme for sixty-nine residential units in five six-storey buildings and five two-storey links was the result of an IBA competition in 1981. Given the same budget and the same spatial requirements, the five German practices proposed different design solutions to the same problem. 'Passive' energy-saving measures include high thermal insulation, triple glazing, solar panels and winter gardens as thermal buffers. 'Active' measures include heat recovery, heat pumps and ceramic stoves. A system of monitors records the internal temperatures and energy costs for each building. These data, together with the general living quality offered by each design, will enable useful comparisons to be made. Unfortunately, little has been made of this information and the architecture does not inspire.

IBA southern Tiergarten

68 Residential Buildings beside the Kulturforum
1984–85
Hilzigallee 17–21, Sigismundstrasse,
Tiergarten
Kurt Ackermann

This block of seventy-five residential units with underground parking recognises IBA's concern for encouraging an inner-city mix of private and public functions. Sitting on the edge of the Cultural Forum with its collection of extraordinary buildings, Ackermann's housing provides a welcome contrast by way of its direct strategy and domestic scale. The comb-shaped plan creates three raised open courts sitting a half-level above the street. Strict orthogonal geometry and smooth white rendered surfaces recall the earlier works of Gropius or Mies. Enclosed loggias provide winter gardens on the south-west corner of the four legs and the raised courts are delightfully landscaped as private gardens. This combination of regular geometry, soft greenery and small scale proves very successful.

IBA southern Friedrichstadt

Friedrichstadt, once a central part of the old imperial capital, was almost completely destroyed in 1945 and divided in two by the Wall in 1961. Part of the late seventeenth century expansion of the medieval city, southern Friedrichstadt was laid out in 1732 by Philipp Gerlach, chief city architect to King Friedrich Wilhelm I. The Baroque street plan imposed an order of strong geometry with Friedrichstrasse as its central north-south axis terminated by the 'Rondel' at Hallesches Tor, the southern city gate. The damage caused by the war, the closing down of the great railway stations, Potsdamer Bahnhof and Anhalter Bahnhof **74**, and the building of the Wall in 1961 all combined to marginalise the area. The street pattern and historic character were largely disregarded by the construction and planning schemes of the post-war period.

The IBA initiative of 1979 had to respond to large gaps in the urban structure, isolated large buildings and widened roads, remnants of post-war planning schemes and unused wasteland bordering the Wall. IBA's concept of critical reconstruction of the city focused on a dialogue between historical continuity and contemporary theoretic and artistic expectations. The decision was taken to respect and preserve the historical elements of the urban structure, taking into account the functional changes of the area. The main aims were to mix residential use with work, recreation, social and cultural facilities. Decentralisation was adopted to form a closer link between housing areas and ancillary amenities. The basic urban block structure was preserved whilst dividing large blocks up into more manageable units and orientating apartments to both the courtyard and the street.

69 Residential Building 1984–85
Köthener Strasse 39–43, Kreuzberg
Hans Christian Müller

Köthener Strasse forms the boundary between southern Friedrichstadt and the Potsdamer area which is presently being developed. Müller's building repairs the gap in the street frontage and reinforces the dual aspect of the block with additional buildings behind. A connection between the two parts is made by a full-height atrium containing the circulation. Entrance doors and kitchen windows open off access galleries under the glazed pyramid roof. The space, which is open to the south, is a focus for communication particularly with the elderly and handicapped. The six-storey orange rendered street façade is divided by vertical sections of red brick and semi-circular balconies which provide strong contrasting rhythms to the surviving adjacent blocks.

IBA southern Friedrichstadt

70 **Residential Building** 1988–89

Köthener Strasse 35–37, Bernburger Strasse
16–18, Kreuzberg

Oswald Mathias Ungers

Ungers shows no fear in taking his rationalism to its
most extreme with this corner block. IBA described
the scheme as a 'block within a block' or 'a building
within a building'. It could also be described as a
square within a square. The footprint reveals eight
square plans which rise in the shape of cubes to
support the square perimeter block above. Three-
storey gateways allow access to the central 'square'
with its single tree. The mix includes apartments,
maisonettes and penthouses assembled together
with the ingenuity of the Japanese Puzzle or Rubik's
Cube. White painted mullions on the four-square
windows contrast sharply with the dark brown grid
of clinker brick which is carried through to the inside
of the block. The adjacent children's playground
also uses the square theme in its layout.

71 **Residential Complex** 1985–87

Bernburger Strasse 22–26, Dessauer Strasse
9–14, Kreuzberg

*Christoph Langhof; Borck, Boye, Schaefer; Rolf
Rave; Grötzebach, Plessow, Ehlers*
Ecological concept by Ökologischer Stadtumbau

Increasing concern for environmental pollution and
waste of natural resources prompted this experimental project in an urban context. A total of 106
residential units, integrated with an existing building, complete two sides of the perimeter block. The
five- or six-storey street frontages display a predominance of light rendered surfaces articulated by
bands of coloured tiles. Langhof's building (upper
illustration) terminates the block at its southern
edge in a sharp point by an acutely angled gable.
Raised terraces, loggias and balconies enjoy the
south and west orientation on to the rural landscape
of the block interior. Trees, shrubs, reed beds and
ponds create a wetlands biotope. Domestic sewage passes through a biological treatment plant to
be collected in a central pond where it is augmented
by rainwater which has been filtered through grass
roofs. The treated water is piped back into the
apartments to be used in toilet cisterns and thereby
reducing the waste of drinking water. Organic waste
is composted for garden use and household refuse
is collected in separate containers so that glass,
paper, metal and plastic can be recycled.

The use of vegetation on this urban site as an
alternative to large-scale technological purification

systems was only made possible by extensive residents' participation. This involved an early supply of information, instruction programmes and on-going consultation.

Block interior with wetlands biotope

72 Residential Complex on Mendelssohn-Bartholdy Park 1987–90

Dessauer Strasse 22/23, 25–26a
Schöneberger Strasse 5–13
Hafenplatz 1–3, Kreuzberg

Josef Paul Kleihues; Peter Brinkert; Gernot Nalbach, Johanne Nalbach, Haus Rucker Co; Georg Kohlmaier, Barna von Sartory

The wedge-shaped city block between Dessauer Strasse and Schöneberger Strasse is bisected by a curved pathway linking up the adjacent blocks. The building by Kleihues, director of IBA, defines the north side of the path which is expanded into a 'pocket park'. His design follows the tradition of building up to the neighbouring blank gable with single aspect apartments. Circulation is kept to the rear alongside a narrow vertical lightwell which contains lift shafts and bathroom cores. Continuous ribbons of balconies accentuate the curved façade looking south across the 'park' to the child day-care centre (1990) by Peter Brinkert. This two-storey curved brick building is entered from the north and opens out to the quiet protection of the block interior to the south.

Block by Josef Paul Kleihues

The fragmented nature of the existing block structure has encouraged a variety of architectural responses to the reconstruction. At the southern end of Dessauer Strasse, the building by the Nalbachs follows a Post-Modern pattern with axial symmetry and tripartite layering capped with a 'Corbusian' inspired flying roof. Its white stucco contrasts with the brown brickwork of the two neighbouring buildings to indicate different concerns. The corner building by Kohlmaier and von Sartory, which overlooks Mendelssohn-Bartholdy Park, retains the expression of late nineteenth century industrial architecture. Its slender brickwork frame maximises the potential for increasing the glazed area which incorporates active and passive energy measures. The other

Block by Gernot Nalbach, Johanne Nalbach

building by Haus Rucker Co continues the expression of the brick frame carrying a regular pattern of domestic windows within the recessed panels.

IBA southern Friedrichstadt

73 **Anhalter Park Primary School** 1987–90
Schöneberger Strasse 23–32, Kreuzberg
Wolfgang Scharlach, Rainer Wischhusen

New schools and day-care centres are part of the IBA plan to provide ancillary amenities for the incoming residents to the area. Subject of an open competition in 1984, this prize-winning scheme by Scharlach and Wischhusen provides teaching facilities for 390 pupils with a sports hall and outdoor spaces. The plan displays a concern for differentiating between functional requirements which are 'ordinary' and 'special'. A regular two-storey brick block addresses the street and three fan-shaped blocks open out to the views of the park. The two-storey street façade of well-mannered brickwork binds together the three elements of fan-shaped large classrooms, smaller classrooms/ancillary spaces, and the shed roofs of the sports hall.

74 **Anhalter Bahnhof (Ruined Remains)**
1876–80
Askanischer Platz 6–7, Kreuzberg
Franz Schwechten

Unlike many other German cities, Berlin did not have one central station. Like London or Paris, several major stations served as termini to the numerous lines which converged from different points of the compass. Anhalter Bahnhof occupied an important location at Askanischer Platz a short distance from Potsdamer Platz **56**, the city's commercial hub. The Potsdamer Bahnhof, constructed earlier in 1872 was limited in size by its constricted site. The Anhalter's newly found status, therefore, was suitably expressed by an imposing architectural front of arched windows and colonnades. Six platforms, which received trains from Paris and Moscow, were enclosed by a large vaulted roof with paired bowstring trusses, impressively engineered in slender steel. Although damage during the Second World War saw the removal of the roof, the station remained in service with its main walls standing until 1952. Despite much protest and debate during the 1950s, the building was finally demolished in 1961. Only the portico was spared as a monument to the city's railway heritage.

75 Residential Corner Block 1994
Stressemannstrasse 109, Dessauer Strasse 40
Zaha M. Hadid

Overlooking the site of Martin Gropius Bau **76** stands an imposing eight-storey corner block by Hadid, part of an IBA residential complex of 140 publicly subsidised units. IBA guidelines asking for an average of five-storey development were felt inappropriate in this area of buildings of different types and periods. The required density was achieved by a long three-storey block terminating in an eight-storey tower on the corner. The acute angle of Stressemann-strasse and Dessauer Strasse is well suited to the architect's repertoire of facets, angles and sharp corners. She exploits the drama of the site by cantilevering the residential accommodation over the corner shop and access route to the courtyard. In design terms the approach is reminiscent of her 1986 competition entry for Adenauerplatz where the visual detachment of the upper section of the block is a central theme. The textured metal cladding reflects the light like fish scales adding another dimension to the expression of the block.

76 Martin Gropius Bau (former Museum of Applied Arts) 1877–81
Stresemannstrasse 110, Kreuzberg
Martin Gropius, Heino Schmieden

The Kunstgewerbemuseum (Museum of Applied Arts) was sited to the north-eastern corner of Prinz Albrecht Palace gardens (since destroyed). It faced north to the newly established Prinz-Albrecht-Strasse (now Niederkirchnerstrasse) and before the Second World War was flanked by the Völkerkundemuseum (German Folklore Museum) to the west and the Kunstgewerbeschule (School of Applied Arts) to the east. It was the school building that the Gestapo commandeered as its headquarters and the recent excavations revealed underground prison cells which are now accessible as part of the exhibition 'Topography of Terror'. All three were extensively damaged during the war, but fortunately Martin Gropius Bau has been retained for its architectural merit. Part of the Berlin Wall ran down Prinz-Albrecht-Strasse cutting off the front entrance and placing the building in a difficult position until 1979 when restoration began. The building is now back to serving its original purpose as an art gallery and museum, with its main entrance now on the south side. Internally a large central top-lit hall is surrounded by a vaulted gallery which provides access to the rooms. The well-mannered exterior of decorative brickwork reflects the late nineteenth century's interest in Italian Renaissance referring also to Schinkel's Bauakademie, 1832–35 (since destroyed).

IBA southern Friedrichstadt

77 **'Die Mauer' ('The Wall')** 1961–89

Niederkirchnerstrasse, Kreuzberg/Mitte

Ehrhardt Gisske

Following the Second World War, the joint Allied administration agreed upon definite sectors of occupation for the four powers: the Soviets in the East and the French, British and Americans in the West. In 1953, repressive Communist rule combined with shortages and rising prices led to an uprising in the Eastern sector.

Relations between the two Germanys deteriorated as large numbers of East Germans fled to the West. On the morning of 13 August 1961, the Eastern authorities laid out barbed wire fences and interrupted the city train lines in an attempt to stem the flow. A few days later work on a more permanent construction began. West Berlin became an island, enclosed by fortifications, isolated within the Soviet-controlled German Democratic Republic (GDR). Access to the West was possible only by a limited number of road, rail and air links. Within the city, checkpoints controlled the limited access for foreign visitors between East and West. The total length of the Wall was 155 kilometres (97 miles) of which 45 kilometres (28 miles) ran between East and West Berlin and the remainder between the GDR and West Berlin. Over the years the design of the wall was 'improved' to consist of two parallel walls on either side of a 'death strip' patrolled by border guards and guards dogs overlooked by 300 watchtowers. Despite these measures, 5,043 people managed to flee to the West with 3,221 arrested in the attempt. Of the eighty people who lost their lives, sixty were shot by the GDR border guards.

The root causes of the GDR's problems, however, resurfaced again in the 1980s. When Erich Honecker proved unresponsive to Mikhail Gorbachov's reforms, fresh floods of East Germans left the GDR for the West via Poland, Hungary and Czechoslovakia. Massive public demonstrations resulted in the Wall being opened in November 1989. Much of the Wall has now been removed, its precast concrete sections broken down and recycled into road construction. Only small areas remain as monuments, the graffiti-covered western face chipped away by trophy hunters and street traders.

78 Residential Tower and Self-Built Terraces
1988

Wilhelmstrasse 119–120 Kreuzberg

*Pietro Derossi (tower); Dietrich von Beulwitz
(Terraces)*

Berlin, in line with many other cities, has a tradition for using towers to emphasise the corners of the block. Increasing the height and freeing the building from the constrictions of the historic context, allows the tower to gain a symbolic meaning, providing a point of identity and orientation for the area. The twelve-storey residential tower by Derossi of Turin articulates the top six floors as being visually separated from the base which is integrated into the rest of the block. A further delineation of the top five floors is made by adding a white rendered finish on the north and east sides to that of the red brick. The celebratory elements of masts and awnings on the roof suggest the special experience of living in and, at the same time, above the city.

The self-build terraces are the result of a concept by Dietrich von Beulwitz. Built against a south-facing blank gable, the reinforced concrete framework of stepped terraces enables tenants to occupy a variety of spaces with the opportunity of extending. Much of the fitting out was carried out by the tenants under professional supervision.

The north-eastern corner of the block, at the junction of Wilhelmstrasse and Anhalter Strasse, is reinforced by another twelve-storey **residential tower** (1988) by 'Grupo 2c' from Barcelona. More regular in its form and less free in its expression, it continues the concept of emphasising the corner of the block and forms a dialogue with the Derossi Tower.

79 Residential Building 1988

Kochstrasse 1–5, Wilhelmstrasse 39,
Kreuzberg

Aldo Rossi

Winner of a restricted international competition in 1981, the project was Aldo Rossi's first major commission outside Italy. eighty-three residential units, community rooms and three shops form a seven-storey block which respects the alignment of the street and reinstates part of the old perimeter block. A play is made of combining large- and small-scale elements. Small square windows contrast with large square windows which in turn are part of a larger square group. Along Kochstrasse, a regular series of ground floor colonnades creates a permeable street frontage of shops and community rooms. With a reference to Filarete's Column in Venice, Rossi marks the corner with a giant white column which also protects the diagonal access into the block interior. The steep triangular roofs of the circulation towers pierce the skyline and divide the façade into sections consisting of brick towers alternating with curtain walling. These divisions are further expanded in Wilhelmstrasse by glazed winter gardens which protect balconies from the road noise. The continuous systematic use of red brick, articulated by twin bands of yellow ceramic, contrasts with the white stucco of the courtyard façade. Overall Rossi succeeds in providing the block with a life and vitality which extends beyond a pure play of forms.

IBA southern Friedrichstadt

80 Residential and Commercial Complex
1988–91

Kochstrasse 67–75, Wilhelmstrasse 40–42a,
Zimmerstrasse 1–10, Kreuzberg

Martorell, Bohigas, Mackay; Pfeiffer,
Ellermann; Schürmann;
Grashorn, Flammang, Licker; Faller,
Muschalek, Schröder; Bartels, Schmidt-Ott

The urban redevelopment of this derelict block
exploits the different condition of its three sides.
The buildings to the south enfront the busy
Kochstrasse facing across to the Rossi block **79**.
The Wilhelmstrasse frontage includes a gateway
building to connect the interior of the block to the
park planned on the former Prinz Albrecht Palais
site. The Wall ran along Zimmerstrasse which
necessitated pulling the northern edge back to
allow access. This building by Bartels and Schmidt-
Ott also contains a gateway, once framing a view
of the Wall but now connecting the court with
Zimmerstrasse. The building is uncompromis-
ingly modern with white rendered smooth surfaces, square modular windows, and interlocking
rectangular and cylindrical forms.

Residential block by Bartels and Schmidt-Ott

The gateway building by Pfeiffer and Ellermann,
while continuing this modernist white architecture, reflects an earlier more heroic period. Pilotis,
curved balconies and stepped sections combine
to add drama to the central opening which is
bisected by a mast and line of neon lighting.

Residential blocks by Martorell, Bohigas and Mackay

The southern edge to the block consists of
three buildings which enfront the street linked
by the gables of three gatehouse buildings
which form spurs into the block interior. The
street buildings by Faler, Muschalek and
Schröder provide a horizontal emphasis by
stepping back the upper three floors of white
stucco above three floors of brick. Continuity is
provided by the third-floor gallery which extends across the gatehouse buildings by
Martorell, Bohigas and Mackay where a single
steel post provides structure and signals entry. A vertical tower of glass blocks combines
with a curved roofed gable to project above the
neighbouring eaves and provide a separate
gable identity on the street for these courtyard
buildings. The architects take full advantage of
the quiet interior of the block in planning the
orientation of rooms and raised terraces. Plinths
are delineated by polychromatic ceramic brickwork and the sculptural roof forms suggest a
special attic living opportunity.

81 Luftfahrtministerium (Air Ministry Headquarters) 1935-36

Leipziger Strasse 5, Wilhelmstrasse, Mitte
Ernst Sagebiel

Since the mid nineteenth century, the area around Potsdamer Platz had been populated by members of parliament and government officials. They were followed in the early part of the twentieth century by major government bodies such as the Chancellor's Office, Foreign Office and Ministry of Justice. Albert Speer's new Chancellery (1938) for Hitler stood nearby in Voss Strasse.

Under the National Socialists, the 'Heimatstil' - a romanticised pitched-roof vernacular - became the style of the people, whereas a sterile version of Romantic Classicism - calling more on the heritage of Gilly, Langhans and Schinkel - became the style of the state. Sagebiel's Air Ministry, like his Tempelhof Airport 112 and Werner March's Olympic Stadium 140 are survivors of the intended 'Thousand Year Reich'. Robust construction and hard enduring materials of steel, limestone and granite combine with minimal articulation to provide the cold impersonal physiognomy. As with the other two buildings, the scale here is also impressive and is a testimony to the importance placed on civil and military air travel in those early years.

82 Residential and Commercial Building 1987-89

Friedrichstrasse 207-208 (Checkpoint Charlie), Kreuzberg
Elia Zenghelis, Mathias Sauerbruch, Rem Koolhaas

Prizewinner of an international competition in 1981, the building was originally designed for thirty-one residential units and border facilities for the Allies and West German customs at Checkpoint Charlie. With the opening of the Wall on 9 November 1989, the ground floor functions were rendered obsolete and were subsequently reconstructed as shops. Architecturally, the regularity of these showcase boxes lacks the variety of the original assemblage which played off against the regular horizontality above. Set back from the street front to shield the occupants from a view of the Wall, the primary orientation for the housing is to the interior of the block. Above a podium of shops, maisonettes sit on an 'elevated garden' level with three floors of small apartments above accessed by an open gallery. On top is a deck of penthouses under the alloy wing roof perforated by circular openings. Architecturally, while this cross-section reveals a conscious attempt to develop a new solution for housing, the façade, with its enforced changes and ribbon windows, is less successful.

IBA southern Friedrichstadt

83 Residential and Commercial Building
1982–86

Kochstrasse 62–63/Friedrichstrasse 43
(Checkpoint Charlie), Kreuzberg

Peter Eisenman, Jaquelin Robertson

Historically, the junction of Kochstrasse and Friedrichstrasse had always been a lively place. During the Cold War, the special significance of Checkpoint Charlie and the proximity of the Wall became critical generators in this competition-winning design. The original unrealised concept enveloped most of the block in a 3-D network of surface, walls and boxes to engage with the Wall along the north edge. The angular geometry results from superimposing the Mercator grid over the Baroque street pattern. This rotational shift is translated on to the building in a composition of columns, planes and stripes. The cantilevered top two floors add drama to the corner while the De Stijl colours of the Mondrian façade provide a graphic memory of the original concept. Along with thirty-seven residential units and a large shop, the building houses an extension to the 'Checkpoint Charlie Museum'. This permanent exhibition documents the detailed history of the Wall with poignant reminders of escape attempts, both successful and unsuccessful.

84 Mosse-Zentrum Media Centre 1995
(Originally the **Mosse Publishing House** 1921–22)

Jerusalemer Strasse, Schützenstrasse, Mitte

Erich Mendelsohn; Jürgen Fissler and Hans-Christof Ernst

The Rudolf Mosse publishing house occupied a late nineteenth century building which was damaged in the street riots of 1919. The owner, impressed by the newly published design drawings of the Einstein Tower **175**, commissioned Erich Mendelsohn to renovate the building. The design work, also involving the young Richard Neutra, resulted in a remodelling which incorporated two existing façades, two additional storeys and created the renowned Art Deco corner.

The building suffered extensive war damage and the site lay dormant from 1961 because of its position within the no man's land of the adjacent Berlin Wall. The recent reconstruction has tried to stay true to the Mendelsohn original. The Jerusalemstrasse 19th century façade which had not survived has been replaced by a new stone section - complimentary to the original without pastiche - which balances the composition and revives the spirit of the original.

85 North Ritterstrasse Residential Complex
1982–88

Above and below: gateway buildings, Rob Krier

Ritterstrasse 55–60b, Lindenstrasse 30–31
and 36–37, Alte Jakobstrasse 120a–121
Feilnerstrasse 1–4 and 18–15, Oranienstrasse
99–105, Kreuzberg

*Rob Krier (including the masterplan);
Dietrich Bangert, Bernd Jansen,
Stefan Scholz, Axel Schultes;
Barbara Benzmüller, Wolfgang Wörner;
Axel Liepe, Hartmut Steigelmann, Eckhard
Feddersen, Wolfgang von Herder;
Joachim Ganz, Walter Rolfes; Klaus Kammann;
Urs Müller,
Thomas Rohde; Jasper Halfmann, Clod Zillich
(landscape design)*

One of the earliest and most coherent examples of IBA's urban planning objective to reinstate the inner city as a place to live goes back to basics. The perimeter block carves out a hierarchy of spaces. The street, the square and the courtyard define public, semi-public and private territory. Apartment buildings on the block perimeter are based on the tradition of being individual but adjoining. Orientation to both sides enables the tenants to relate to the street life as well as to the quiet block interior.

Adopting Krier's masterplan, an invited competition to fourteen Berlin architects ensured a variety in the buildings for 314 residences, thirteen shops and underground parking for 210 cars. The ground plan connects four continuous blocks, with their private courts, to a central square - Schinkelplatz - accessed by short avenues. The southern side of this public space consists of the reconstructed façade of Feilner House, built in 1828–29 by Schinkel for the local manufacturer

Building by Ganz and Rolfes

of clinker bricks. Two existing office buildings were upgraded and incorporated into the block, the 'Merkur' building (1910) by Curt Leschitzer and the former 'Reichsschuldenverwaltung' both now serving as government offices. The latter, by Bestelmeyer is a distinguished red brick structure from 1924, its vertical rhythm of brick piers and terracotta panels reminiscent of works by Poelzig or Höger.

The red brick continues on the smooth gently curved façade of the neighbouring five-storey building by Ganz and Rolfes with eight bays of brick piers limited to the first three floors of the central section. Like the older building, the courtyard elevations use white stucco for its economy and light reflective qualities.

A set of gateway buildings, arranged in pairs, create a link between the courtyards across the short avenues. The exterior staircase and access galleries within the opening are protected from the weather by glass roofs. The four-storeys consist of two maisonettes with the uppermost adopting a studio character.

Special attention was given in general to the design of shared entries and stairway halls in recognition of the influence they have on the way residents identify with each other and their building. Balconies within the block interiors provide a more intimate connection with the space which is given a different character in each court. Trees, pergolas and trellis work separate surfaces of grass, gravel and sand to provide spaces for relaxation, play or just walking the dog.

Courtyard

On the south side of Ritterstrasse, the four-storey building by Krier signals access to the rear of the block by stretching the gateway into a long low arch. Two side wings provide a balanced asymmetry to the axial opening by varying the composition of loggias, balconies and windows. The structural spine, terminated by a small double balcony to the street, is decorated by a sculpted figure to the courtyard. The predominance of light grey stucco is relieved by coloured columns, balconies and window frames in the Post-Modern tradition.

86 Residential Complex 1987
Lindenstrasse 81–84, Markgrafenstrasse 5–8, Kreuzberg

Herman Hertzberger

This impressive work solves a difficult planning problem with simple elegance. Occupying the central section of a broken triangular perimeter block with a church at its tip, the 'D' plan form plugs the gap, turns the corner and creates two new courtyards. The curved three-storey section leaves the church free to stand apart and rises to five-storeys as it connects with the two existing six-storeys to terminate the block. The straight three-storey section provides a link which creates an 'old' court to the north and a 'new' garden court to the south, connected to each other through a stairway. Five more entrance stairways allow access to the garden and rise as glazed 'vertical walkways' linking the apartments with

Courtyard

their basement parking and roof terraces. Guarding the entrances are symmetrical clusters of overlapping balconies, their adjacent fenestration blending both function and artistry. The garden and children's playground provides a central focus for the community and, despite its intimate scale, enjoys good daylighting. A co-operative association of tenants was involved in the early design stages and continue to administrate the forty-eight apartments. Hertzberger, assisted in Berlin by Inken and Hinrich Baller, shows a great attention to detail while only using reinforced concrete, white stucco and pale green metalwork. The design succeeds on many levels and is a testimony of the architect's pursuit of a humane modernism.

87 Residential Buildings with Studio Tower
1986–88

Charlottenstrasse 96–98, Kreuzberg
John Hejduk, Moritz Müller

IBA's 'critical reconstruction of the city', which concentrated on integrating different pieces of architecture into an urban design concept, also found a place for the mavericks. In his writings and drawings Hejduk has always resisted the idea of regionalism, preferring a more enigmatic approach. Two five-storey structures extend from the existing block forming an open square with a freestanding fourteen-storey tower in the centre. A variety of one-, two- and three-bedroom apartments are arranged under the butterfly roofs of the low buildings which present their 'faces' to the street. Seven two-storey studio apartments make up the main tower with its four attached service stacks of lift, stair, kitchen and bathroom. South faces are rhythmically demarcated by metal awnings and balconies. The Braque-inspired Cubist palette of grey, black and green, also used on Hejduk's Tegel Villa **106**, conveys an aura of melancholy.

IBA southern Friedrichstadt

88   Residential Park by Berlin Museum
1984–86

Lindenstrasse 15–19, Alte Jakobstrasse 129–136, Kreuzberg

Hans Kollhoff, Arthur Ovaska (including the masterplan); Werner Kreis Peter Schaad, Ulrich Schaad; John Eisler, Emil Prikryl, Jiri Suchomel (Stavoprojekt) Franz C. Demblin; Horst Hielscher, Goerg P. Mügge; Arata Isozaki; Jochem Jourdan, Bernhard Müller, Sven Albrecht; Dieter Frowein, Gerhard Spangenberg

Urban villas

Block by Kries and Schaad

Kollhoff and Ovaska's prizewinning urban concept divided the site into three parts: the existing museum **89** with its new park to the south, a transitional zone with two rows of urban villas and a courtyard development at the rear of the Viktoria Insurance building to the north. The complex consists of a total of 320 residential units, built under the state-subsidised housing programme, with parking for 150 cars (predominantly underground). A new private road separates the linked row of urban villas from the courtyard block and a network of pathways and restricted routes connects the open spaces and provides access to the parking. The density is increased from the detached villas through the linked villas to the perimeter apartments which extend the traditional pattern to the north. A series of green spaces are complementary to this sequence from the new park of the museum through the linear gardens of the villas to the 'copse of acacias' in the courtyard which had grown up on the post-war wasteground.

Kollhoff and Ovaska's linear building

One row of five-storey urban villas is paired with another row consisting of two blocks of three with two-storey links. Variations on a theme are played by different architects with exterior design and internal layouts. A mix of apartments and maisonettes expand into the metal-clad roofs whose geometry reflects the Baroque roofs of the museum's rear wings. Red brick plinths and entrance porticoes stand out against the pale grey stucco which is further relieved by a sprinkling of small coloured elements. Pergolas and planting bring order to the linear garden and raised terraces occupy the roofs of the two-storey links.

The seven-storey building by Kries and Schaad provides a formal street frontage for the villas and transitional façade between the Viktoria building and the Berlin Museum **89**. It does this with a self-assurance and panache which, avoiding pastiche, employs symmetry and tripartite layering in a powerful composition with a projecting central

section with flanking balconies. The red brick wall incorporates several 'fragments' from the destroyed buildings and is topped by a bronze metal flag.

The southern section of the perimeter block consists of a linear building by Kollhoff and Ovaska connected to the Viktoria building by a corner 'tower'. Placed against the existing blank gable, its slenderness is due, at least in part, to its single aspect plan. Along its length, independent and parallel planar systems are developed to express the building's volumetric and structural imagery. Recessed planes of white stucco are mastered by layers of solid red brick in an attempt to reconcile the 'modern' and the 'traditional'. In the centre of the seven-storey building is a gateway defining a cross-axis to the new road and linking the park with the block interior. As a focal point to this pedestrian route is an eight-storey tower which translates the same language into a vertical statement. Differentiating front and back results in a more direct use of white stucco to the courtyard which evolves to include balcony towers on the adjacent buildings by Frowein and Spangenberg.

Separating the large court with its children's playground and existing copse from a small court at the rear of the Viktoria buildings is the new building by Isozaki. Built in 1906–13 by Wilhelm Walther for the Viktoria Insurance Company, the original building had a monumental façade 130 metres long and twelve courtyards. Of the surviving parts, the Lindenstrasse frontage best illustrates the architectural megalomania of the period. Isozaki's Post-Modern contextualism responds to the three remaining sandstone façades of the old court in several ways. Relating to the tripartite, the first two floors are given a rusticated base, the next three floors share the more regular paired window pattern of the piano nobile, and the top floor is broken by gable articulation. Colour and materials offer contrast with warm grey precast concrete 'stone' cladding, pink and cool grey stucco and window walls with horizontal transoms. The dark painted recessed window surrounds on the upper floors coincide with the larger openings to overlay the traditional wall with the expression of a gridded frame, more

Block by Arata Isozaki

characteristic of Isozaki's other works. Rising to meet the roofscape, the 'frame' supports two of the architect's most favoured element, the vaulted roof. Returning to the ground, the building reaffirms its contextual roots by using a recovered sandstone pedimented doorway as a portal to the main entrance.

89 Kollegienhaus (Berlin Museum)
1734–35

Lindenstrasse 14, Kreuzberg
Philipp Gerlach

Gerlach, chief city architect to Friedrich Wilhelm I, was responsible for planning Southern Friedrichstadt which was laid out between 1732 and 1738. The Kollegienhaus originally housed the offices of the Royal Judiciary and the Supreme Court. Designed in the style of a nobleman's residence, it was the first administrative building of its kind in Berlin. The Baroque style had developed during this period into a national Prussian style exemplified here by the architect's capable handling. The design shows similarities to the Kronprinzenpalais (1732) on Unter den Linden, originally by Gerlach and subsequently altered by others. Symmetrical ramps, a feature of Berlin Palaces, lead up to an entrance portal which displays the symbolic figures of Justice and Mercy over the pediment. Despite being severely damaged, the building was restored after the Second World War and since 1969 has housed the Berlin Museum with a collection illustrating the history and culture of Berlin.

To the rear of the building lies a public green space, and IBA theme park by Hans Kollhoff and Arthur

Ovaska, completed in 1988. Gerlach's original design provided a large garden corresponding to the ministerial gardens which formerly belonged to the palaces of the nobility on nearby Wilhelmstrasse. The design provides a contemporary interpretation of a Baroque garden laid out to include a trellised walk, topiary work, lawns, water channel with fountain and a terrace with poplars.

IBA southern Friedrichstadt

90 The Jewish Museum 1992–96

Lindenstrasse 9–10, Kreuzberg

Daniel Libeskind

Although not strictly an IBA project, the idea originated as a further development of IBA urban strategy for the area. It was subject of an international competition in 1988–89 for an extension to the Berlin Museum **89** including a Jewish Museum on the vacant site to the south. Libeskind, well known for his theories and various competition entries, has been given here a significant opportunity to put his intellectual theories into practice. Although much of the design was evolved during its constructional phase, the original 'lightning' plan and much of the splintered deconstructivism remains to make its mark. Considering its context, this is a building of enormous scale, measuring more than 10,000 square metres and having no fewer than 365 windows. Although the design exploits the depth of the site, south of Kollhoff and Ovaska's park, the street frontage remains monumental. The museum reintegrates the history of Berlin with Jewish history, uniting the two across the void created by the Holocaust. This 'void' is represented spatially, by five voids and six voided sections, cutting though the building's angular geometry as a metaphor for the absence of Berlin's Jewish citizens.

91 Cultural and Leisure Centre for the Deaf with Residential Accommodation 1990–94

Friedrichstrasse 10–15, Kreuzberg

Douglas Clelland; Maedebach, Redeleit; Joachim Schmidt; Walther Stepp

There has been an advisory centre and meeting place for Berlin's 4,000 deaf people at number 12 Friedrichstrasse since 1976. It was founded and developed by the deaf themselves as a self-help project. In 1983, three architects were commissioned by IBA to extend the project over three plots with Joachim Schmidt advising on the upgrading of the existing building at number 12 which dates from 1898. A small gateway building at number 13 leads to the new primary school by Valle, Broggi and Burckhardt at the rear of the block. The school has a special facility for children with speech difficulties.

Friedrichstrasse façades

The three new buildings on Friedrichstrasse contain about forty residential units, some with special facilities and a commercial area of about 600 square metres. The high-ceilinged ground floor continues the existing street pattern of shops while the linked first floor provides communal rooms for groups, counselling and festivities. Apartments in the upper floors include supervised dwellings for deaf and handicapped young people.

Above: recreational park; below: Thomas Weissbecker Haus

Directly across Friedrichstrasse, the **recreational park** was completed in 1990 by Poly and Pfannenstiel following an IBA competition. The gable murals at the west side of the park belong to **Thomas Weissbecker Haus**, 1987, a communal residence for homeless young people. Architects Mott and Schöning worked with the building's occupants for this self-help project to create four communal units each for eleven people with café, workshops and offices on the ground floor.

92 Deutscher Metallarbeiter Verband (Metal Workers Union Building) 1929–30
Alte Jakobstrasse 148–153, Kreuzberg
Erich Mendelsohn

This building, together with the destroyed Columbushaus office building on Potsdamer Platz (1931–32) represents the last in a series of major buildings in Berlin by Mendelsohn. Like the Cinema Universum Complex **37** on the Kurfürstendamm, this building was originally conceived as part of a larger urban plan. The surviving re-entrant curved façade would have extended across Lindenstrasse to meet another elongated block curving around into Gitschiner Strasse. When this extended block was deleted, Mendelsohn's sketch studies reveal an exploration of the remaining corner where a variety of vertical elements play off against the horizontal emphasis of the flanking façades. The final built form, however, reverts to the horizontal ribbon windows and spandrel panels of the original composed to provide the nautical imagery of a ship's 'bridge' and 'mast' flagpole. The use of metal, glass and travertine are carried into the interior with its poetic staircase of sweeping curves and tubular handrails. The design embodies the language of 'Neue Sachlichkeit' with the expressionistic genius of Mendelsohn. In 1933, the unions were banned and the home of the Metalworkers, like other union offices, was taken over by the Nazis. During the same year, as a result of death threats, Mendelsohn emigrated and the city lost one of its most original and inventive architects.

Corner block, Kreuzberg, 1982–84, Hinrich Baller, Inken Baller 93

IBA/STERN Luisenstadt, SO36

In 1840, Peter Joseph Lenné, the royal director of gardens, was commissioned by the King of Prussia, Friedrich Wilhelm IV, to draw up a plan of 'ornamental and peripheral boulevards in Berlin and surroundings' in order to create an attractive expansion of the city. The plan created for Luisenstadt, to the east of Friedrichstadt, included numerous squares and a new waterway, the Luisenstadt Canal, which linked the River Spree to the Landwehr Canal. Originally built to attract industry the canal survived until 1926 when it was eventually filled in. The building development which first took place consisted of low perimeter blocks with only sheds and workshops in the internal courts. This density increased throughout the century with higher apartment blocks and overdevelopment of the courts. The changes into a working-class area created the 'Kreuzberg mix', a dense combination of living accommodation and light industry described at the turn of the century as the 'largest city of tenements in the world'.

The area to the east of Luisenstadt, known as SO36 (its postal district code), followed on a similar pattern of development. Originally part of James Hobrecht's plan of 1862 for extending Luisenstadt, the ground plan was realised rapidly, at low cost with fewer squares and parks. Workers streaming in from Silesia were housed in overcrowded conditions around the Görlitzer Bahnhof which by the start of the First World War had become one of the most deprived working-class districts of Berlin.

Levels of damage sustained during the Second World War varied with some parts surviving almost undamaged. Several urban renewal plans of the 1950s and 1960s including motorways, industry and high-rise blocks of flats were debated, altered and finally dropped in 1976.

Careful repair and renewal of these seriously run down and derelict districts became the IBA approach starting in 1979, which was then taken over in 1986 by STERN (The Gesellschaft der behutsamen Stadterneuerung Berlin mbH). This involved intensive participation by local people in conserving the building fabric and retaining the social and economic structure of the community. The special character of the 'Kreuzberg mix' was retained with careful alterations to the ground plan only where necessary. Decisions regarding urban renewal were agreed by planners, inhabitants, business and trades people. Public facilities such as streets, squares and green areas have been renewed and extended.

93 Residential Complex 1982–84

Fraenkelufer 26, 38–44, Kreuzberg

Hinrich Baller, Inken Baller

In 1975 this curved perimeter block overlooking the water and grassy banks of the Landwehr Canal was under threat by proposed changes to the road network. Once this threat was removed, the IBA competition of 1979 involved the partici-pation of the residents in formulating proposals on how best to rebuild the block structure. Three gap sites were infilled with new buildings on the curved perimeter and a long single-aspect block is built against the gable wall of the adjacent property in the internal court. A total of eighty-seven new apartments were created and a fur-ther 200 existing units in the block were reno-vated. The Ballers apply their own individual architectural language, varying the theme be-tween the two gateway buildings, the corner building and the courtyard building. Tilted rein-forced concrete pilotti express the structural frame, sharp-pointed curved balconies enjoy the southern orientation and the inverted boat roof forms recognise the potential of attic living. The landscaping of the court is romantically rural and the Fraenkelufer riverside walk is linked to the green strip of canal embankment.

See also illustration page 86

94 Self-Help Projects in Admiralstrasse
1984–86

Admiralstrasse 15–20, Kreuzberg

Kjell Nylund, Christof Puttfarken, Peter Stürzebecher et al.

Several self-help projects have been successfully developed in Admiralstrasse under the auspices of IBA/STERN. Seven of the blocks were old building renovations and one new building project. In 1980 the unoccupied buildings were awaiting demolition to make way for a new road until the 'Instand-besetzer' (resto-squatters) moved in. Shortly after-wards they formed themselves into a housing asso-ciation, one of the first in Berlin since 1945, and set themselves up as a teaching building site. The conversion and renovation work was carried out to a high standard by the residents and the gap at number 16 was infilled by a new block of apart-ments, maisonettes, balconies and roof terrace. The construction was organised in a close co-operation between architects, planners, builders and future residents. A reinforced concrete frame-work enabled the owners to create their own envi-ronment 'living in a shelf unit'. The variations of timber cladding and glazing used on the façade is unified by a gridded layer of steel balconies.

95 Residential and Commercial Renewal 'Wassertor' 1979–89

Wassertorplatz, Erkelenzdamm, Kohlfurter Strasse, Kreuzberg

Evans, Goschel, Haupt, Rebel, von Rosenberg

Some of the original squatter mentality is evident in the defensive appearance of this renovation. The curved elevation to Wassertorplatz with its twin towers and steel ramparts resembles a fortress. The project was a forerunner to IBA with the self-help renovation by the residents taking ten years to complete. The block houses forrty-four apartments, seven shops, a café and restaurant with its own diesel generator in the basement helping with energy requirements. Recognised as a pioneering project by the Berlin Senate, the project received generous grants much to the envy of similar self-help groups in the area. The open gable of the block displays a bold glazed wall with its steel framework of balconies supporting greenery.

96 Residential and Commercial Building 1979–85

Reichenberger Strasse, Mariannenstrasse, Kreuzberg

Wilhelm Holzbauer; Rolf Rave

When IBA became involved with this triangular site in 1979, almost all of the original block had been pulled down to make way for an earlier development plan. The Viennese architect Holzbauer and his Berlin contact Rave proposed a new planning solution based on an adaptation of his 'Wohnen Morgen' complex in Vienna. One hundred and two residential units, two shops and an underground car park address adjacent streets, envelop two existing buildings and connect with a corner building. Strong cubic forms of red brick are decorated by patterns of blue glazed brick, varied to give a different identity to each of the repetitive stair towers. The top two floors of the six storeys are 'screened' from the street behind a metal mesh supporting greenery. White painted stucco is the predominant finish of the block to the rear which steps to accommodate raised gardens, terraces and glazed verandas.

IBA/STERN Luisenstadt, SO36

97 Residential and Commercial Building
1910–11, 1978–79
Kottbusser Damm 2–4, Kreuzberg
Bruno Taut; Hinrich Baller, Inken Baller

The building sits south of the Landwehr Canal, over the bridge from Luisenstadt/SO36, and although not part of the IBA its renovation sets an interesting precedent. Built by Taut only three years before his futuristic Glass Pavilion and subsequent involvement with the utopian ideals of the 'Glass Chain' group, the design owes more to the 'Kunstwollen' (Will to Form) of the Deutsche Werkbund. Here with the recessed balconies, attic ribbon windows and mannered decoration can be seen the exploration of ideas which achieved such success with Taut's social housing schemes for the Gehag during the 1920s. After the Second World War, the building lay in ruins until its renovation in 1978. The Ballers took the unconventional approach of retaining only the front section of the block - one room deep - and reconstructing a new section to the rear court.

This creates a cross-section with old room heights to the street and lower modern room heights to the rear. Each apartment, therefore, 'enjoys' various changes of level. The architecture to court continues the Ballers' free form expressionism found across the canal at Fraenkelufer **93**.

98 Housing Rehabilitation 1984–87
Adalbertstrasse/Waldemarstrasse, Kreuzberg
Beisswenger, Domin; Kamke, Knöfel; Meyer-Rogge et al.

The typical Luisenstadt block structure laid out in 1840 by Peter Joseph Lenné can be found in the area north of Kottbusser Tor. In 1926 the canal, which bisected Luisenstadt, was filled in and now serves as a linear park running between the two former basins of Wassertorplatz to the south, and Engelbecken to the north.

The careful urban renewal organised by IBA and its successor STERN involved preserving the outer appearance of the streets, demolishing many buildings in the interior of the blocks and modernising some buildings involving the application of new building standards. The replacement of old buildings by new was minimised and all work progressed only with the continued involvement of local people.

Where the decorative stucco had been knocked off and replaced by smooth render, new friezes and murals by local artists have been incorporated into the renovations. The corner of Adalbertstrasse and Waldemarstrasse was decorated by the Turkish artist Hanefi Yeter. The renovated façades of Adalbertstrasse serve as a reminder of the elegant boulevards originally planned by Lenné in the mid nineteenth century.

99 Spreewaldbad (Municipal Swimming Baths)
1984–87
Spreewaldplatz, Kreuzberg, SO36
Christoph Langhof

This area, known as SO36, which had undergone rapid growth during the last half of the nineteenth century had always been deprived of social amenities. Following various unrealised plans for the site of the demolished Görlitzer Bahnhof, it was decided to form a landscaped park and build a swimming pool. The complex includes saunas, water cascades and a large pool with waves. Langhof brings the element of fun into the architecture by a bold expression of the structural frame and a flat roof covered by a myriad of 'bubbles' in the form of plastic domed rooflights. The eccentric structure of gold-painted steel trusses, suspended from the apices of short rocker columns precariously poised on checkerboard cylindrical plinths, certainly requires a second look. The building grows out of a hill which is part of the park and the use of internal planting with large areas of glass curtain walling reinforces this link with the surrounding landscape.

100 Residential Building 'Bonjour Tristesse'
1982–83
Schlesische Strasse 1–8, Kreuzberg, SO36
Alvaro Siza Vieira

The typical Kreuzberg block structure of SO36 can be found in this area north of the new park occupying the site of the former Görlitzer Bahnhof. Streets such as Soranerstrasse, Oppelnerstrasse and Falkensteinstrasse contain the tenements which at the turn of the century were cramped, overcrowded, badly ventilated and unhygenic. Even today, the typical apartment consists of two rooms and a kitchen with half of those having to share a toilet on the landing. Nevertheless, tenants are keen to stay and IBA has taken on the challenge of converting tenements into low cost housing by installing toilets and bathrooms, increasing space standards, repairing façades and brightening up the yards. The north-eastern corner of Falkensteinstrasse and Schlesische Strasse was the subject of a limited competition in 1980 to renovate and repair the block. The winning scheme by the Portuguese architect consisting of a sympathetic conservation and a bold new building contains forty-six apartments, five shops, an old people's day centre and a day nursery. Siza Vieira's sweeping curved façade attempts to avoid architectural pastiche by linking the existing blocks as directly as possible. Despite user participation the block was labelled 'Bonjour Tristesse' by the inhabitants.

IBA Prager Platz

IBA Prager Platz

The district of Wilmersdorf was established in the 1870s along the road between Charlottenburg and Potsdam. The entrepreneur J.A.W. von Carstenn acquired the 'Deutsch-Wilmersdorf' estate in order to build a 'town of exclusive villas in the English style'. His urban plan used the Kaiserallee (now Bundesallee) as the north-south axis with symmetrically arranged ornamental squares, such as Prager Platz, balanced on either side. Although the ground plan survived, the 1895 development plan resulted in a change from the garden city character in favour of spacious apartment blocks constructed on the Parisian model. Hermann Muthesius, who favoured the English model, claimed to be perplexed as to why this move towards apartments proposed by the 'least educated' elements of the population could ever have been accepted by the 'most educated'. Nevertheless the palace-type apartment blocks completed around Prager Platz in 1907 continued the language successfully established around the Kürfürstendamm nearby.

101 Residential and Commercial Buildings
1989–92
Prager Platz 1–12, Prinzregentenstrasse 1–16, 96–97 Trautenaustrasse 23–24, Wilmersdorf
Gottfried Böhm, Rob Krier, Klaus Kammann, Carlo Aymonino

Extensive damage during the Second World War resulted in piecemeal development to the area during the 1950s and 1960s. Following planning proposals for the square by Carlo Aymonino, Rob Krier and Gottfried Böhm in 1977, IBA adopted Böhm's strategy to retain the historic urban ground plan and reinterpret the architectural expression. The revitalisation of the square and the addition of public amenities are intended to upgrade the quality of the neighbourhood. Lack of funds and numerous political and legal obstacles have still to be overcome before the IBA concept can be fully realised.

The central space retains the simplicity of the historic design of a grassy oval with a central fountain. Unfortunately the adopted traffic scheme is not so simple with two of the five radial roads being 'bollarded' and traffic prevented from driving around the square. Böhm's development on the north-western edge of the square uses a drum and turret bound together by a curved square grid of yellow tiled concrete. Krier's eight-storey circular tower expresses a continuous ribbon of balcony at the fifth floor and is capped by a faceted conical roof. At present, however, the architecture defining the square is too fragmented and additional blocks are required to complete the restoration of this important urban space.

IBA Tegel

Tegel

Situated in the north-west next to Lake Tegel, on the edge of a large expanse of forest, this former village on the Hamburg Road has grown into an important centre for shopping and recreation. During the eighteenth and nineteenth centuries Tegel was better known for the estate of the Humboldt family until Borsig, the machine and locomotive firm, established itself in 1896. One of the city's largest gasworks was built in 1902 and the harbour with industrial rail connections was established six years later. After the Second World War the harbour lost its industrial function except as a landing stage for pleasure boats. Preserving the natural resources of forests and lakes has become a priority for the whole city. The lakes used extensively for recreation serve also as the city's reservoirs.

IBA concentrated on two areas with the redevelopment of the harbour as a residential, cultural and recreational area on one side of Karolinenstrasse and the construction of the phosphate elimination plant on the other. Both areas were subject to restricted architectural competitions in 1980 with the American Charles Moore winning the first and the Austrian Gustav Peichl the second.

Moore's prizewinning masterplan allows the Tegel landscape to play a dominant role, using water to link the residential, cultural and recreational components. The existing harbour has been upgraded and extended with a new island providing a central focus. An open plaza of curved stepped terraces leads to the water's edge and links with the lakeside promenade and tree-lined *allees* between the blocks. During the planning process, Moore had to revise his concept several times, but the final form remains true to the original. A total of 351 apartments are housed in a variety of serpentine blocks - echoing the curved shoreline to the north - and seven urban villas - providing a regular edge for the street to the south. Together with the work of Moore and his associates are projects by three other Americans, and architects from Rome, Paris and Berlin.

02 Residential Complex 1987
Am Tegeler Hafen, Tegel, Reinickendorf
Masterplan by Charles Moore, John Ruble, Buzz Yudell

Four curved blocks are arranged in such a way that their gables form an octagonal courtyard defined by four 'houses' and four gates. The axis through these gates links landscaped gardens with open commons and ends with views of the harbour and forest. Moore's block steps up from five storeys to eight, its zinc-covered roof forming a community of dormers and loggias which exploit the views. The design employs Post-Modern Classical motifs which bring a degree of variety to the precast concrete building system.

IBA Tegel

103 Humboldt Bibliothek (Humboldt Library) 1988
Am Tegeler Hafen, Tegel, Reinickendorf
Charles Moore, John Ruble, Buzz Yudell

Part of the cultural complex, planned to include
an adult education centre, music school and
multi-purpose hall, the library was completed in
1988. The informal grouping of buildings is
intended to capture the spirit of waterfront
warehouses. Moore gives the library a more
formal appearance and succeeds in making it
both monumental and intimate. The factory
roof lights and extruded cross-section have an
industrial look which sits uncomfortably with
the neo-Classical ordering and arched gable
windows. The entrance is celebrated with a
post and lintol arch intended as a homage to
the nearby Schloss **109** designed by Schinkel
for Wilhelm von Humboldt, after whom the
library is named. The interior contains large-
scale gestures with small intimate spaces.
Light from above floods through the open wood-
slatted vaulted ceiling on to arcaded galleries of
tall bookshelves and high entrance foyer with its
circular control desk. Contrast is provided by the
reduced scale of the children's library and the
quiet lounge with its fireplace and club chairs.

104 Residential Terrace 1987
Am Tegeler Hafen, Tegel, Reinickendorf
*Regina Poly, Karl Heinz Steinebach, Friedrich
Weber*

The Berlin architects Poly, Steinebach and Weber
created the four-storey curved block extending
to the east of the octagonal court. Their design
continues Moore's Post-Modern Classicism in a
more muted way. Base, middle and top are given
a more rigid expression and the metal roof is cut
by a regular pattern of roof terraces.

105 Residential Terrace 1987
Am Tegeler Hafen, Tegel, Reinickendorf
*Dietrich Bangert, Bernd Jansen, Stefan Scholz,
Axel Schultes*

This Berlin practice has been responsible for
several projects in other IBA areas. Here they
have two four-storey curved blocks woven into
the Moore masterplan, one to the west of the
octagonal court and the other continuing the
Poly, Steinebach and Weber block **104**. With the
exception of the gable expression, they take a

more rational approach with square perfora-
tions, smooth surfaces and cylindrical stair
towers penetrating the metal roof.

106 Urban Villas 1987–88

Am Tegeler Hafen 15a–18, Tegel, Reinickendorf
*15a John Hejduk; 16 Antoine Grumbach;
16b Paolo Portoghesi;
16c Stanley Tigerman; 16d Robert Stern;
18 Charles Moore, John Ruble, Buzz Yudell*

John Hejduk, Dean of Cooper Union's School of Architecture, New York, has a reputation as an educator and theorist. He has also designed another IBA residential development with a studio tower **87** in Southern Friedrichstadt. Hejduk's Tegel villa, located at the western end of the street, takes a bold reductivist approach. Paired volumes capture the essence of the generic house form anchored by the central staircase 'chimney'. Simple elements such as square windows and porches contrast with the extraordinary light scoops on the roof. The grey render and dull green paintwork combine to convey a rather bleak appearance.

15a Villa by John Hejduk

Antoine Grumbach, the Parisian architect, takes a formalistic approach showing concern for platonic geometries: the drum and the cube, the circle and the square. This exercise in granite-clad abstraction contrasts with Moore's general theme for the development.

16 Villa by Antoine Grumbach

A certain amount of anonymity is shared by the neighbouring villa by Paolo Portoghesi from Rome. Basic mono-pitched forms and simplistic fenestration rely too heavily on colour - yellow stucco with orange edges - for identity.

Stanley Tigerman takes a more playful approach to the picturesque. Inspired by historic precedent, the gable and dormer are adopted as a repetitive element. The building is cut in half by a glazed stair hall or winter garden symbolising the division of East and West. A further association with Berlin is made by colouring the steel, checkerboard tilework and stucco in the red, black and orange of the German flag.

16b Villa by Paolo Portoghesi

The New York architect Robert Stern, well known for his private houses, seems quite comfortable with the Moore strategy. For inspiration he draws upon the turn of the century villas and mansion houses found in Tegel and other areas of the city. Baroque influences can be seen in the roof form and the curved dormers. Wrought-iron railings and tile-decorated stucco demonstrate an attention to fine detail, exemplified by the 'star' motif along the soffit of the eaves as a play on the architect's name.

16c Villa by Stanley Tigerman

IBA Tegel

The largest of the villas, set back from the street, serves as a link block between the villas by Stern and Moore. Berlin architects Poly, Steinebach and Weber compose a symmetrical assembly with a central block flanked by side wings. The stark marble-clad grid of the central section is echoed in the two free-standing portals half engaging the side wings. Appearing like a stage-set for abstract modern rationalism, the frontage provides a strong contrast to its two neighbours.

The villa to the eastern end of the street plays a pivotal role by also addressing the stepped radial entry plaza. The design by Charles Moore and his associates expresses best their ideals of Post-Modern Classicism. The motif of post and lintol predominates, both as a free-standing portal or pilasters and cornice. The symmetrical arrangements and tripartite order given to all four façades are noticeably more successful on the villa than on the five to eight storeys of the curved block.

16d Villa by Robert Stern

16c Villas by Poly, Steinebach and Weber

18 Villa by Charles Moore

107 Phosphateliminierungsanlage PAE (Phosphate Elimination Plant) 1982–85

Buddestrasse, Tegel, Reinickendorf

Gustav Peichl

The purpose of this plant is to remove phosphates from water contaminated by industry and sewage farms which threatens the biological balance of the lakes. The plant, located beside the River Nordgraben, processes the water and purifies it before allowing it to flow into the lake and piping it to a fountain in the new harbour extension. Peichl avoids the anonymous architecture of the industrial shed by adopting the iconography of the ship with a scale and articulation which relates to the adjacent residential area. The building sails on a sea of green pushing ahead of it a great bow-wave containing three flocculation tanks arranged in a triangle over-looked by the 'ship's bridge'. This symbolic expression of technology introduces a new spirit to Berlin's industrial architecture, ironically, by its nostalgic references to the International Style of the 1930s.

108 Residential Building 1987–89

Schloss Strasse 19, Tegel, Reinickendorf
Gustav Peichl

The nautical imagery is carried over to the adjacent residential building by Peichl at Schloss Strasse 19. Built between 1987 and 1989, this IBA project repairs the open end of an existing perimeter apartment block. Peichl deals with the northern orientation by forming three linked blocks, their bow-like curves steering between the PEP **107** and the new harbour to gain the advantage of east-west light.

109 Humboldtschoss 1821–24

Adelheidallee 17–23, Tegel, Reinickendorf
Karl Friedrich Schinkel

The Havel lakes, which so occupied the interests of royalty to the south-west around Potsdam, also extend up to the north-west of the city around Tegel. Since 1765, the Humbolt family had owned an estate in this beautiful hilly area of forests, meadows and vineyards. In the early nineteenth century Schinkel rebuilt the existing castle for Baron von Humbolt, the Royal Prussian State Minister. The existing tower was retained, remodelled and incorporated into the new design with additional towers at each corner to express the character of a castle. The style, although Classical, is highly restrained with decoration kept to a minimum. Sculpted reliefs at the top of the towers representing the eight winds are based on the old wind tower of Andronicus Cyrrhestes in Athens.

110 Borsigturm (Borsig Works Tower) 1922–24

Berliner Strasse 29, Tegel, Reinickendorf
Eugen G. Schmohl

August Borsig, the 'Locomotive King', founded his heavy engineering plant in 1838, the same year that the railway line between Berlin and Potsdam was opened. The firm's reputation for invention and innovation was called on in 1841 when King Friedrich Wilhelm IV commissioned the construction of a steam engine for the Pumphouse **169** which feeds the fountains and waterways of Sanssouci **176**. The Borsig Tower was Berlin's first skyscraper. The high-rise structure, containing office space, is constructed with engineering brick reinforced by a steel frame, the whole faced in ashlar, its verticality interrupted at three-storey intervals by large angular cornices. The expressionist three-storey crown, with its Gothic overtones, provides the tower with its strongest visual characteristic and unique identity.

Residential building, Hinrich and Inken Baller 116

111 Riehmers Hofgarten (Riehmer's Courtyard)
1881–92

Hagelberger Strasse 9–12, Grossbeerenstrasse
56–57, Yorckstrasse 83–86, Kreuzberg

Wilhelm Ferdinand August Riehmer, Otto Moesk

Pressure to increase the density of the perimeter block structure at the end of the nineteenth century often resulted in overdevelopment of the courtyards with overcrowding and unsanitary conditions. The developer and master builder, Riehmer, avoided this pattern by creating a network of narrow streets and intimate green spaces within the block. By effectively turning the block outside-in he improved upon the architectural language of the earlier main street façades and created a quiet, elegant and more private environment. He also had a shrewd eye for attracting a particular clientele: officers of the Dragoon Guards from the nearby barracks. One can picture the scene, like an old hand-coloured etching, of the young Prussian officers in their smart uniforms grouped against these stylish surroundings.

112 Zentralflughafen Tempelhof
(Tempelhof Airport) 1936–41

Platz der Luftbrücke, Tempelhof

Ernst Sagebiel

Berlin's first central airport was created on a military parade ground from the Wilhelminian era. Work was started in 1922, with the terminal building completed by 1929. In the 1930s, Tempelhof became the busiest airport in Europe and the redesign was entrusted to Sagebiel, the architect of the Air Ministry Headquarters **81** in Leipzigerstrasse.

Started in 1936, and planned as a component of Speer's north-south axis, the building was still incomplete although operational during the war. The complex consists of fourteen sections symmetrically disposed about a diagonal axis linking the curved arrivals building with the rectangular urban square. The central hall is a magnificent space flanked by galleries and colonnades but the scale of the overall plan owns more to megalomania than practicality. What did they intend to do with all that office space?

After the war, Tempelhof was at first used as a military airfield, then as a civil airport from 1951 to 1959 before Tegel became the main airport. With the increasing demand for flights to Berlin, it is once more possible to fly in and out of Tempelhof and experience its scale and grandeur at first hand.

Inner suburbs

113 Königskolonnaden (King's Colonnades)
1777–80

Heinrich-von-Kleist-Park, Potsdamer Strasse,
Schöneberg

Karl von Gontard

The structure is a reminder of the old town centre's eighteenth century grandeur. Many of the bridges over the River Spree and its canals were enclosed for protection, flanked on either side by colonnaded sections of road. Shops and market halls occupied the sites behind the colonnades which became important focal points and meeting places. Many were unfortunately destroyed by road widening and new bridge building around the turn of the century. The 'Königskolonnaden', one of the finest to survive, was relocated here in 1910 from Königstrasse (now Rathausstrasse) to make way for a department store. As royal architect, Gontard was responsible for many prestigious works such as the domed churches **23** in the Gendarmenmarkt (formerly Platz der Akademie) and the Neues Palais **180** in Potsdam. A fine example of late Baroque Classicism with coupled Ionic columns and decorative sculpted figures along the parapet, his colonnades have been given a new lease of life and now grace the entrance way to the Kleistpark.

114 Kirche am Hohenzollernplatz (Hohenzollernplatz Church) 1930–33

Hohenzollerndamm 202–203, Wilmersdorf

Fritz Höger

Höger's best-known work, the 'Chilehaus' (1923) in his native Hamburg, became one of the expressionists' best-known images: a sharp-edged ship's prow soaring above the street corner on vertical ribs of masonry. The site here was pressured by two residential street blocks converging to a point on one side and Hohenzollernplatz widening to form an urban square on the other. Höger provides a powerful solution which is monumental to the main road (the square having since been absorbed by the urban motorway) and terminates the residential blocks on the other. The curved end to the nave sweeps round to the angled road and the tower closes the vista of the other. The vertical emphasis of ribbed brickwork on the nave and tower echo the Gothic tradition, but it is the architect's cool expressionism which gives the church such a strong character. Geometry of a different kind also plays a part in the beautiful interior where rainbow-coloured stained glass enlivens the concrete pointed arched structure of the nave.

115 Rathaus Charlottenburg (Charlottenburg Town Hall) 1899–1905
Otto-Suhr-Allee 96-102, Charlottenburg
Reinhardt and Süssenguth

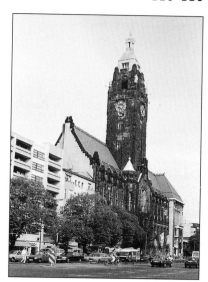

Before it became enveloped by the expansion of Berlin, Charlottenburg was a flourishing town in its own right. At the turn of the century its prosperity could be gauged by the scale of the new town hall completed by 1905. The height of the tower was purely a matter of prestige, vying with that of the Berliner Rathaus **1** and remaining taller than those of the Schöneberg and Spandau town halls. The heavy masonry walls and decorative treatment of the tower reflect the spirit of these times, confident and adventurous. Unlike other prestigious buildings of this era, however, this version of 'Reich Braggadocio' displays a sure-handed combination of Jugendstil and national Romanticism. The stonework combines fine ashlar with heavy rustication and sculptured embellishments. Heavy vaulting, decorated with mosaics and paintings, characterises the ground floor interiors with an elaborate central staircase linking an extension to the rear completed in 1915 by Heinrich Seeling.

116 Residential Building 1985–86
Schloss Strasse 45–47, Charlottenburg
Hinrich Baller, Inken Baller

Schloss Strasse forms a wide tree-lined avenue on the north-south axis of the Charlottenburg Palace **118**. Hebbelstrasse cuts across the avenue on the diagonal, forming an acute-angled intersection which is expressed in the gable of the block. The Ballers carry much of their architectural expressionism here from their new building and infill at Fraenkelufer **93** in Kreuzberg. The two-storey base is defined by large areas of glass behind reinforced concrete 'piloti'. The central section of four-storey rendered façade is broken up by projecting angular balconies with spidery steel balustrading. The inverted boat roof forms of two-storey attics provide the architect's strongest signature: the drama heightened on the gable by the acute angular cut of the side street.

Inner suburbs

117 Sporthalle (Sports Centre) 1987–88
Schloss Strasse 55–56, Charlottenburg

Hinrich Baller, Inken Baller

This is a particularly ingenious solution to the architectural problem of shoehorning a sports centre into a gap site on the residential Schloss Strasse. An Olympic-size sports hall sits above a gymnasium the size of the handball court with both spaces opening themselves out to the street. The building celebrates its function by a clear expression of structure: large spanning floor elements and a slender shell-like Gothic roof with its timber latticework enjoyed internally and visible externally. This relationship of inside and outside is enriched by the articulation of the glass façade which borrows small-scale elements, such as ornamental ironwork, from the neighbouring residential buildings.

118 Schloss Charlottenburg (Charlottenburg Palace) 1695–1712

Luisenplatz, Charlottenburg

Johann Arnold Nering, Johann Friedrich von Eosander, Georg Wenzeslaus von Knobelsdorff, Carl Gotthard Langhans

The district of Charlottenburg, once a flourishing town at the turn of the century, grew out of the medieval village of Lützow. The site to the west of the village, positioned at a bend in the Spree, was chosen by the Elector Friedrich III to build a country palace for his consort Sophie Charlotte which, over the years, was expanded and developed into a summer residence for the Prussian kings. Work was started by Nering in 1695 on a small building with a central pavilion with two wings. By 1701, when Prussia became a kingdom and Elector Friedrich III became King Friedrich I, the Swedish architect Eosander was employed for his experience in the Court of Louis XIV and the scale of the masterplan was increased. Two larger additional wings were planned about Nering's original building which was extended and given a domed tower. Only the long orangerie to the west was completed before the death of the King when work was halted by his son - the Soldier King - who was compelled to implement economies. Building continued in 1740 when King Friedrich II commissioned Knobelsdorff to complete the east wing, symmetrical with the orangerie. The theatre by Langhans in 1790 completed the expansion.

Much of the palace was destroyed by fire following an air raid in 1943 and, since the war, has been slowly restored to the delight of Berliners who enjoy taking long walks through the spacious grounds.

The Schlosspark has undergone many transformations following the various fashions of the day. In 1783 Johann August Eyserbeck altered the original Baroque layout of the regular geometries into a 'nature' park. In 1828, Peter Joseph Lenné applied his principles of the Romantic landscaped garden retaining many of the older features. Following Second World War devastation Joachim Kaiser laid out the park in the spirit of the Baroque original with a small section to the north set aside as a more open parkland by Walter Hilzheimer.

119 Schinkelpavillon 1824–25

Luisenplatz, Charlottenburg

Karl Friedrich Schinkel

Originally known as the Sommerhaus or Neue Pavillon, the building was designed at the same time as the Schloss **159** and the Kasino **160** at Klein-Glienicke near Potsdam and shares the same Italian inspiration. During his grand tour two years earlier Friedrich Wilhelm III had stayed on the coast near Naples in the Villa Reale Chiatamone and on his return commissioned Schinkel to build this copy. The rectangular form, flat roofs and shuttered windows became characteristic of this 'Biedermeier' period of Romantic Classicism. Considering the size of the Schlosspark, the summer-house sits uncomfortably close to the Schloss, providing a stark contrast in scale, style and form. Following interior damage during the Second World War, the building was restored between 1957 and 1970 and now serves as a museum displaying the artistic heritage of Berlin in the first half of the nineteenth century with a significant collection of Schinkel's drawings and paintings.

120 Belvedere 1789–90

Schlosspark, Charlottenburg

Carl Gotthard Langhans

Originally sited on an island in Eyserbeck's 'nature' park, subsequent alterations to the watercourses and the nearby railway embankment have spoiled the original seclusion of the Belvedere and its view to the north. Nevertheless, walking through the Schlosspark, around the lake and over the romantic bridge, it is still possible to enjoy its 'discovery' half-hidden among the trees. The circular tower with its bell-form roof, front portico and two truncated wings incorporates balconies and viewing platforms. The details display an elegance and delicacy from the smooth rustication of the base through the Composite columns and pilasters of the middle to the sculpted window reveals of the top. Langhans' beautiful Rococo pavilion, layered like a wedding cake and painted like sugar icing, still makes a pleasant impact on its surroundings.

Inner suburbs

121 Residential and Commercial Buildings
1982–86

Luisenplatz, Charlottenburg

Hans Kollhoff

The urban plan for these twin blocks reveals a bold concept. The northern block forms a link between the street architecture of Charlotten Ufer and Eosanderstrasse, colliding with, and appearing to slide through, a surviving fragment of nineteenth century apartments. The southern block sits back behind a new three-storey linear block to form a square, curving round to link its gable with the façades of Otto-Suhr-Allee. This strategy is both reverential and provocative, by merging with some existing blocks and creating positive spaces while appearing to crash straight through another. The contrasting approach continues with the expression of materials and architectural elements. Dark clinker brick is used for the solid body of the slender block terminated by subtly curved balconies on the gable. The wing-shaped roof is finished in smooth white rendered surfaces and the curved glazed curtain wall forms a winter garden frontage to the apartments. A total of sixty-five residential units are located in the two seven-storey blocks, which combine to express Kollhoff's confident approach to modernism.

122 Gustav-Adolf-Kirche (Gustav Adolf Church)
1932–34

Herschelstrasse 14–15, Charlottenburg

Otto Bartning

In 1919, Bartning was a member of the 'Arbeitsrat für Kunst' group which included Max Taut, Adolf Meyer and Erich Mendelsohn. Their 'Exhibition of Unknown Architects' of that year expounded the group's ultimate goal of creating the ideal 'Cathedral of the Future' which would encompass everything in one form: architecture, sculpture and painting. More than a decade later, Bartning produced this beautifully harmonic design - its modernism difficult to date - within the gridiron of surrounding nineteenth century residential blocks. A diagonal axis aligns with the street intersection, rising to culminate in the cross on a progressively slender bell tower. From the top of the tower, a series of vertical planes, decreasing in height and widening in angle, enclose the fan form of the nave with its concentric rows of pews. The structure is of reinforced concrete and steel with brick infill. The stained glass, also by Bartning, uses strong primary colours with shades of blue predominating in the panels of the bell tower interior. This effect, unfortunately, is partly lost to the exterior at night by the brick infill necessitated by structural damage during the Second World War. Two symmetrical church buildings terminate the street frontages, relating in scale to the adjacent residential area and forming gatehouses to the courtyard garden at the rear.

123 AEG Turbinenfabrik (Turbine Assembly Hall) 1908–09

Huttenstrasse 12–19, Tiergarten

Peter Behrens

The Deutsche Werkbund was founded in 1907 by ten factory owners and thirteen artists with the intention of improving the form and quality of consumer goods. Between 1907 and 1914, Behrens was employed by AEG (Allgemeine Elektrizitäts Gesellschaft) not only as an architect but as their 'artistic adviser'. As such he was involved in the design of factories, workers' housing, shops, products and company stationery, each calculated to enhance the company's reputation for excellence in the new field of electrical appliances. During this time, Walter Gropius, Mies van der Rohe and Le Corbusier were also employed in Behren's office.

The Turbine Hall is generally regarded as representing a transitional phase of architecture - its roots in the Classicism of Gilly and Schinkel - striving towards a new 'objective' realism. Strong geometric forms and repetitive elements are suggestive of mass production and the machine age. The three hinged portals with beam ties have an apex height of 25 metres. This steel structure, which also supports the linear tracking crane, is clearly expressed along the length of the elongated plan and accentuated by recessing the glazed infill. The gable with its powerful and apparent solidity expresses more 'classical' elements. Two tapering corner pylons, although non-loadbearing, visually 'support' the massive polygonal tympanum with its lettering and company emblem.

From a modernist perspective, the very appearance of load-bearing walls with massively rusticated corners conflicts with the light steel frame and glass infill. Behrens, however, subscribed to the theory of 'Kunstwollen' or 'Will to Form' - along with other members of the Werkbund - style was ultimately more important than technique. Undoubtedly a masterpiece of early industrial architecture, the Turbine Hall survives today as a temple to the early years of the machine age.

The building was lengthened by almost 100 metres in 1939 by Schallenberger and Schmidt, and is one of the earliest industrial buildings to have been listed.

Hinged base of the steel portals

Inner suburbs

124 Doppelinstitut (Centre for Manufacturing Technology) 1983–86

Pascalstrasse, Tiergarten

Gerd Fesel, Peter Bayerer

The centre is shared by the Technical University's Institute of Tools and Manufacturing Technology and the Fraunhofer Institute for Production Plants and Construction Technique ,both with the remit to foster creative technology. Offices, computer rooms and workshops on several storeys are wrapped around the central hall in a concentric three-quarter circle. This white metal-clad circular section protects a large glazed open hall by shielding it from solar gain and exposing it only to north light. The hall, which totals 3,200 square metres and is 14 metres high, is used for experiments. The circular plan form nestles into the curve of the River Spree with the dramatic north façade providing a lively frontage to the river. Comparisons with Behrens AEG Building **123**, which is nearby, are interesting: both use a tracking crane in generating form - one revolving, one linear - and both successfully integrate industrial architecture in an urban context.

125 Tiergarten Sewage Pumping Station 1987

Alt-Moabit, Tiergarten

Oswald Mathias Ungers, Stefan Schroth

This building, like the tip of an iceberg, sits above a subterranean suction pumping station which treats effluent from a 680 hectare area of the city. Above ground, the industrial red-brick building was required to harmonise with its residential surroundings and the old pumping station of 1890. As with some other works of Ungers in Berlin, the original design drawing reveals a bold concept and a clear strategy which promises more than is finally realised. The glazed roof became solid for reasons of sound protection, the chimneys had to be extended to clear the eaves of the adjacent blocks and the greenery on the flat roofs has not yet appeared.

126 Focus Business Service Centre 1987–93

Stromstrasse, Moabit, Tiergarten

Joachim Ganz, Walter Rolfes

The new complex offers a variety of office and production space and is largely occupied by computer and electronic service companies. The site beside the River Spree and the Lessing Bridge was previously occupied by a variety of traditional Berlin industrial brick buildings. Some of the original structures have been adapted to provide points of interest and reference within the new layout of standard solutions. The new architecture utilises mass-produced, terracotta-clad panels which owe more to a abstract preoccupation with square geometry than with the much richer possibilities found in Berlin's great tradition for innovative industrial buildings.

127 Johanniskirche (Johannis Church) 1832–34

Alt-Moabit 25, Tiergarten

Karl Friedrich Schinkel

The church was one of four designed by Schinkel for Berlin during the early 1830s. Originally, there were to have been two large churches before a Royal decree requested that four smaller parish churches be built for the same expenditure as two. The redesign resulted in all four sharing a similar form, to the approval of Friedrich Wilhelm III. A rectangular plan provides a central nave flanked by two subsidiary aisles with choir galleries above and to the rear. Construction and decoration were kept much simpler than originally intended with masonry walls supporting the timber roof structure. The Johanniskirche shares the curved apse decorated with frescos and three stained glass windows with the others. It differs in the design of the ceiling to the nave which excluded horizontal beams in favour of expressing and decorating the underside of the double pitch roof which is supported by curved timber arches: a good example of Schinkel's poetic utility.

In 1853, a growing congregation necessitated various additions by Friedrich August Stüler, a pupil of Schinkel. The resultant ensemble included a school house and a bell tower which were linked to a new entrance and portico by a colonnade. In the 1890s the main church was further extended by Max Spitta.

Inner suburbs

128 Nazarethkirche (Nazareth Church)
1832–34
Leopoldplatz, Wedding
Karl Friedrich Schinkel

Of the four parish churches designed by Schinkel for Berlin during the early 1830s, the Nazarethkirche is the only one to survive in its original form. As with the Johanniskirche **127**, the interior was gutted during the war and has subsequently been restored. The simplicity of construction and decoration owes much to the restriction of the budget which was originally designated for two large churches. The simple rectangular plan consists of a central nave, two side aisles with choir galleries above and a curved apse. The brickwork façades are totally devoid of applied decoration, relying on the pattern of windows and use of proportion for its success. A small, modest construction such as this expresses the essence of Schinkel's architecture: clarity of form, economy in construction, and 'schlichtheit' (unpretentiousness).

129 Residential Block 1971–76
Vinetaplatz, Wedding
Josef Paul Kleihues

Kleihues, who later became planning director of the new building division of the IBA, demonstrates here, in this earlier work, his concerns with urban morphology. Respect for the traditional five-storey perimeter block and understanding the qualities of historic street patterns was further explored by the work of IBA during the 1980s. Community life within the city revolves around the hierarchy of public to private spaces: the square, the street, the courtyard. At Vinetaplatz, the crisp modern street façades are cut back at the corners where high gateways allow a diagonal access to the semi-public garden within the block interior. A limited palette of red facing brick and white timber windows combined with a simple homogeneous design has ensured that the building still looks good and provides a refreshing contrast to many of the later, more 'fashionable' IBA projects.

130 Siedlung Britz, 'Hufeisen' (Britz Residential Estate, 'Horseshoe') 1925–31

Fritz-Reuter-Allee 2–72, Lowise-Reuter-Ring 1–47, Britz, Neukölln

Bruno Taut, Max Taut, Martin Wagner, Eduard Ludwig, Bruno Schneidereit

At the turn of the century, the area to the south-east of Berlin saw a growth of large business concerns which had outgrown the expansion potential of the inner city. These were initially followed by small residential areas and by the 1920s and 1930s some of the best prototypes of the great residential estates were established in this and other cheaper land outside the ring railway. As municipal building surveyor, Martin Wagner had first called for the public running of housing affairs in 1917 which, one year later, was taken up by the city. Bruno Taut gained experience with housing estate projects in Magdeburg where he was city architect from 1921 to 1923. The following year, Taut became adviser to the GEHAG (Gemeinnützige Heimstätten, Spar-und Bau-Aktiengesellschaft) in Berlin.

The Britz was one of the first of this social building movement, closely linked to the trade unions, pursuing an ideological alternative. Social, economic and political ideals were combined with a desire for healthier living with fresh air, sunlight and gardens. The heart of the Britz is characterised by the large horseshoe apartment block enclosing a small park with a central pond. The grand nature of the axial plan is emphasised by the monumental staircase connection to Fritz Reuter Allee, flanked by symmetrical end blocks containing shops and cafés. Taut's masterly articulation of the curved 'wall' incorporates his trademark 'T' formed by the vertical grouping of stair windows and horizontal strip of attic laundry windows on a blue rendered ground in contrast to the predominating white. On the three-storey façade recessed balconies, like opera boxes,

look out over a triple row of private gardens on to the landscaped communal space, providing a safe place for children to play.

Brick is used as surrounds to openings, in vertical strips to frame each section of apartments, and

1 *Bruno Taut*
2 *Max Taut*
3 *Martin Wagner*
4 *Edward Ludwig*
5 *Bruno Schneidereit*

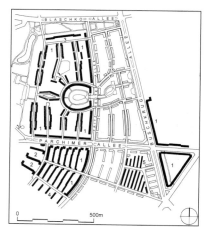

again in larger areas above the additional entries through the curved block. The transition of wall to flat roof is softened by the horizontal punctuation of small square attic windows. Pursuit of the picturesque and considered vistas continues into the small surrounding streets by the use of curves, kinks and staggered rows of terraced houses. Taut creates visual harmony by a unique blend of contrasting elements: pitched pantiled roofs with flat roofs; brightly coloured render with natural brick; formal planning with the picturesque.

131 Siedlung Siemensstadt (Seimensstadt Residential Estate) 1929–32

Goebelstrasse 2–122, Jungfernheideweg 1–45, Siemensstadt, Charlottenburg

Hans Scharoun, Walter Gropius, Hugo Häring, Otto Bartning et al.

The growth of the Siemens factory complex and the general shortage of housing in Berlin were the two main factors which led to the building of this large-scale estate. Situated to the north of the factories, the shared rail link formed its southern boundary with new stations providing a link to the city centre. Six architects, all members of 'Der Ring' (the Ring Group), were chosen to collaborate on the design. Scharoun, responsible for the overall planning and several buildings, built a group of apartments south of the railway line as an entrance to the estate. This block, known as 'the battleship', bristles with nautical images.

Apartment block by Hans Scharoun

Curved concrete shields to balconies, semi-circular windows and cowlings contribute towards this streamlined International Style. Most of the four-storey linear apartment blocks run north/south in parallel rows, each architect seeking to bring identity to the façades by varying balconies, staircases and fenestration.

In a slight departure from this schematic ground plan, both Scharoun and Weber consciously vary

1	Hans Scharoun	5	Fred Forbat
2	Walter Gropius	6	Hans Henning
3	Hugo Häring	7	Hans Hertlein
4	Otto Bartning	8	Werner Weber

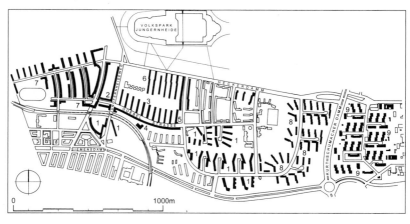

Apartment block by Hans Hertlein

the angle of their blocks. Hertlein contrives to run his blocks across the adjacent streets in three places forming large arched openings. These 'gateways', however, do not celebrate the transition from the street to the courtyard as with the earlier Viennese models or Rob Krier's IBA housing, **57** and **85**.

Gropius treated the rear elevations most severely, concentrating mostly compositional elements to the front overlooking the shared gardens and children's playgrounds. White rendered walls are broken up by the use of brick on balconies with glazed projecting stair towers sectioning off the façade. Bartning brings a certain quirkiness to the expression of small,

narrow, horizontal windows - for the attic laundry rooms - neatly compressed up under the eaves. His cantilevered balconies of steel and brick are of such slender dimensions as to look extremely fragile. The predominance of white render, shared by most blocks, is varied most by Häring. His extensive use of natural brick introduces warm colours and decorative articulation in various patterns. Curved reinforced concrete balconies with brick parapets form rows of suspended gardens and the top laundry floors are expressed in brick to contrast again with the white render. The most severe of the blocks by Bartning, following the long gentle curve of the railway, became known as 'the long misery'.

132 Zitadelle (Citadel) 1560–94

Am Juliusturm, Spandau

Christoph Römer, Rochus Guerrini Graf zu Lynar

Evidence would suggest that fortifications on this strategically important site date back to the twelfth century. The present buildings date back to 1560–94, with later alterations and additions. It was Graf zu Lynar who, after fleeing to Berlin from France during the first Huguenot per-secutions, directed the construction of the star-shaped ramparts. The deep bastions could withstand cannon fire with the geometric plan enabling the main walls to be overlooked, and thereby protected, by the projecting corner bastions. Further protection was achieved by the surrounding moat, flooded by

the waters of the adjacent Havel. Over the years various alterations and additions have taken place including the restoration of the circular Juliusturm (Julius Tower) in 1834 supervised by Karl Friedrich Schinkel.

Outer suburbs

133 Gartenstadt Staaken (Staaken Garden City) 1913–17
Am Heideberg, Torweg, Staaken, Spandau
Paul Schmitthenner

In his book *Tomorrow: A Peaceful Path to Real Reform* of 1898, Ebenezer Howard proposed a concentric garden city ringed by a railway with houses and gardens encompassing a central park. In 1907, Barry Parker and Raymond Unwin developed the diagram into the picturesque layout of Hampstead Garden Suburb.

In Staaken, built originally for the workers of the nearby armaments factory, Schmitthenner takes the basic elements of private gardens, houses, streets, main square with shops and church and sets them out like a model village. A variety of scale is carefully engineered with single family houses of one and two storeys, multi-occupational blocks of three storeys, and apartments above arcaded shops of four storeys. The materials are limited to red brick, buff render, painted timber windows and black or red Dutch tiles. A blend of expressionist brickwork, Dutch gables, Arts and Crafts dormers, bay windows and flower boxes creates a cosy village atmosphere. Although Schmitthenner combines these charming clichés with a great deal of expertise, such sentimentality would be challenged a decade later in the Siedlungen by Bruno Taut and others.

134 Funkturm (Radio Tower) 1925–26
Messedamm, Westend, Charlottenburg
Heinrich Straumer

A hall for the Berlin Radio Exhibition of 1924 was first built by Straumer using timber construction and copper earthing to avoid interference with radio waves. Before the hall was destroyed by fire in 1935, the Funkturm had been completed in 1926 and rendered redundant by 1932 due to its inadequate height as a transmitter. Despite its modest size - 138 metres compared to the 335 metres of the Eiffel Tower in Paris - it became an emblem for the city during the 1930s, and has remained a favourite attraction for generations of Berliners with its restaurant and viewing platforms.

135 Internationales Congress Centrum ICC
1973–79

Messedamm, Westend, Charlottenburg
Ralf Schüler, Ursulina Schüler-Witte

Towards the end of the 1960s, West Berlin was becoming a popular centre for cultural, academic and political visitors. With increasing self-confidence, it was decided to compete with the best international venues for conferences and exhibitions. The new building, adjacent to the Funkturm **134** and old exhibition halls of 1937 by Richard Ermisch, is linked by a pedestrian bridge over the motorway access which leads to parking for 630 cars. The complex provides a congress hall with 5,000 seats, a banqueting hall for 3,000 people, seven halls ranging in size from 150 to 350 seats, press centre, restaurant, dressing rooms and cloak-rooms. Electronic signboards direct visitors through this labyrinth to their desired destination. All these internal functions are packaged together like an overblown electronic machine into a superblock with engineering pretensions. The silver aluminium skin contributes to the inevitable 'spaceship' analogies. Berliners, however, prefer the nickname 'Quasseldampfer' (Chatter-box Steamboat).

136 Haus des Rundfunks (Broadcasting House)
1929–31

Masurenallee 10–14, Westend,
Charlottenburg
Hans Poelzig

During the late 1920s Poelzig was already one of the older generation, a respected teacher who, unlike Gropius or Mies, never sought a completely new architecture or to impose his ideas on others. His spectacular masterpiece and last fully expressionist work was the Grosses Schauspielhaus of 1919 in Berlin, with its cavernous dome and arches of cascading stalactites. Since only small fragments of this interior survive, within what is now the Friedrichstadt Palast, the Broadcasting House is his most important building remaining in the city. The first radio broadcasts in 1923 came from the Voxhaus in Potsdamer Strasse. By 1927 it became clear that a new, larger special building was required, sited logically, adjacent to the Funkturm **134**. Poelzig's design was selected from the subsequent competition and built in three phases, totalling 30,000 square metres. The design was originally conceived as part of a large-scale exhibition complex, knows as the 'Poelzig Egg', which involved a collaboration with the chief city architect Martin Wagner. A curved triangular plan of perimeter offices encloses three broadcasting halls and four courtyards radiating from the central entrance hall and grant staircase. The main axis, which would have bisected the 'Egg', sets up a symmetry of the plan and orders the 155 metre long street frontage on Masurenallee.

This main façade displays an assured formalism with its great length counterbalanced by a rhythmic pattern of vertical piers. The subtle variation of dark-coloured glazed bricks and metal windows adds an enigmatic quality to the building.

Outer suburbs

137 Doppelvilla Heymann-Mendelsohn 1922
Karolingerplatz 5–5a, Westend, Charlottenburg
Erich Mendelsohn

Positioned at the intersection of two streets, the double villa occupies a corner site overlooking a small square. The design of each villa is mirrored by the diagonal axis which bisects the central corner of the block and cuts across the public space. Staggering the form of the block to present three corner 'towers' to the square exaggerates the idea of mass while at the same time placing the dark brickwork above the light stucco contradicts this impression. This helps to create the dynamic tension continually sought by Mendelsohn. His characteristic horizontality, although less apparent, is expressed by the ribbed brickwork of the upper levels and linked windows which zigzag over the folded façade.

138 Haus Sternefeld 1923–24
Heerstrasse 109, Westend, Charlottenburg
Erich Mendelsohn

Like the double villa **137**, the Sternefeld house also occupies a corner site. In this context, the house is held back from the busy main road sitting closer to the quieter side street and incorporating a variety of walls to define external space. The importance of the diagonal view, however, can still be found in Mendelsohn's sketches which show his exploration of massing by sliding and twisting cuboid volumes in search of a dynamic asymmetric composition. The windows are grouped as recessed ribbons, compressed by the strong, uninterrupted wall planes concealing the roof garden. Dark brick surrounds to the windows and openings reinforce the idea of contrasting solid and void in an abstraction of elements. At the same time, a link to the past is achieved by the material use of clinker brick and vermiculated stucco, textured by dragging the stone aggregates.

139 Unité d'Habitation, Berlin version 1956–59
Reichssportfeldstrasse 16, Westend,
Charlottenburg
Le Corbusier

Built as part of the 1957 Hansaviertel Housing Exhibition **43**, Le Corbusier's Unité was inexplicably cast adrift and surprisingly located in the suburbs. New visions of the city as a social and architectural entity where large apartment blocks were surrounded by wide green open spaces were central to Le Corbusier's proposals for 'Plan Voisin' and 'Ville Radieuse'. The Hansa project exemplifies this idea. Le Corbusier designed several variations of the Unité with the Marseilles block (1946–52) being the best known by virtue of its many radical ideas. Held above the ground on huge piloti, this self-contained community contained two floors of shopping midway up the building, health clinics, hotel rooms and a roof terrace with kindergarten, restaurant, gymnasium and running track. Many of these facilities are missing in the Berlin block which despite accommodating 400 families only has a small shop and post office on the ground floor. The key aspect of the design, however, still remains with the cross-section of the block revealing two-level, double height apartments interlocking about a central access corridor every third floor. The Berlin block appears to enjoy a higher level of maintenance than the Marseilles original with bright bold colours adding identity to the double and single height balconies. The 'Modulor' system of dimensions is shown in sculptural relief at the entrance as a reminder of the Le Corbusier concerns with 'harmonious measure' and proportioning to a human scale. Despite this, the predominant ceiling height of 2,260 millimetres seems too low and the overall height of the block too high. Alterations to the design were forced on Le Corbusier by the Berlin authorities during its construction, including additional floors and the removal of the roof terrace. Although flawed, the enormous scale of the block ensures a strong sense of presence, though unfortunately, without much of the Marseilles block's 'Esprit Nouveau'.

140 Olympiastadion (Olympic Stadium)
1934–36

Olympischer Platz, Trakehner Allee, Westend, Charlottenburg

Werner March

This site was occupied by an earlier stadium where a plan to expand the facilities for the 1916 Berlin Olympics had been abandoned because of the First World War. When Berlin was chosen to host the 1936 Olympics a new plan was drawn up expanding the Reichssportsfeld to include an open air theatre, seating 20,000; an assembly area for 500,000; and a main stadium seating 120,000. March's original design, a steel frame with lightweight cladding, which expressed a 'modern' image, met with Hitler's strong disapproval. Speer intervened, had the steel clad in masonry, and added the curved colonnade. The significance of Hitler's involvement in the project and the stadium's impressive logistics were not missed by the Nazi propaganda machine. Although the scale of the stadium is vast, its height is deceptively low due to the depressed level of the playing field. In cross-section the point of arrival from outside leads directly through to the elliptical circulation route which occupies the mid point of the raked seating, providing access both upwards and downwards. This route is ringed by restaurants, cafés and toilets on one side and open to the playing field on the other. Two Mero space-frame canopies, recently installed to provide partial cover for spectators, look incongruous and temporary against the solid monumentality of the arena. The colonnaded perimeter, containing stairways and galleries, connects to the parade ground with its 77 metre high bell tower. Although the structure is steel, generous amounts of limestone cladding and granite paving give an air of strength and permanence intended by the 'Thousand Year Reich'. Black and white images of the 1936 Olympics, captured in Leni Riefenstahl's documentary, are brought to life by the inscribed wall plaque which records the three gold medals won by Jesse Owens, the coloured American who defeated Hitler's Aryan supermen.

Outer suburbs

141 Two Modern Movement Villas 1928

Am Rupenhorn 24–25, Pichelsberge,
Charlottenburg

*Hans Luckhardt, Wassili Luckhardt, Alfons
Anker*

The brothers Hans and Wassili Luckhardt were with 'Die Gläserne Kette' (the 'Glass Chain') from its beginnings in 1919. The group, which included Gropius and Scharoun, was founded by Bruno Taut to exchange ideas on spiritual theories by way of chain letters. The fragile 'Chain' was soon broken when Hans Luckhardt recognised the incompatibility of free forms and rational prefabrication. The move towards a more functional and objective style was explored at the Berlin Secession Exhibition in 1923 and fully established by the formation of 'Der Ring' (the Ring Group) in 1925, which included Mies and Häring. The Weissenhofsiedlung Exhibition of 1927 in Stuttgart, although not involving the Luckhardts, brought together the works of Corbusier, Stam and Oud with the German architects Mies, Gropius, Scharoun, Behrens and Taut. Adopting new constructional systems of steel frame or reinforced concrete structure enabled revolutionary ideas unburdened by history or tradition. The white, cubist, flat-roofed mode of building became the International Style. With the two villas at Am Rupenhorn, the Luckhardts pioneered the use of a steel frame with structural concrete block infill which, despite the 'Corbusian' imagery, sets them apart from the 'domino' frame examples. The spirit of the age is clearly expressed in this heroic new architecture with its concerns for new materials, new forms, sunlight and fresh air.

142 Haus Mendelsohn 1929

Am Rupenhorn 6, Pichelsberge, Charlottenburg

Erich Mendelsohn

Mendelsohn's own house is poised dramatically on the edge of a steep sloping site enjoying views over Lake Havel. Compared to his work of the early 1920s there is a surprising simplicity and directness with both form and materials, reflecting more the influence of 'Neue Sachlichkeit'. Privacy is ensured by distancing the house from the street and restricting fenestration to a high ribbon window for the bedroom area. The informal landscape of the steeply sloping, wooded garden to the lakeside contrasts with the linear formality of the garden to the street. A system of walls, pathways and changes of level, starting at the street entrance, envelop the house with a variety of outdoor spaces which connect the house to the site and provide a link with nature.

143 DLRG Rettungsturm (Life-Saving Association Training Facility) 1969–72

Am Pichelssee 20–21, Pichelsdorf, Spandau

Ludwig Leo

Leo applies his lateral thinking to the problem of accommodating thirty boats, workshops, information gathering facilities, classrooms and bedrooms on a limited site of expensive lake-side land. The triangular tower incorporates a diagonal elevator on the angular façade reaching a height of 30 metres which lifts boats from the canal for storage in a high-rise boat park. The building also incorporates a first aid facility and diving chamber where depths of up to 158 metres can be simulated. As with Leo's other work there is a peculiar blend of logical reasoning, individuality and fun. Constructivism meets Archigram!

144 Haus Baensch 1934–35

Höhenweg 19, Weinmeisterhöhe, Gatow,
Spandau

Hans Scharoun

With his house in the Weissenhofsiedlung Exhibition of 1927 in Stuttgart and the Schminke house of 1933 in Löbau, Saxony, Scharoun originally embraced the ideals of 'Neue Sachlichkeit'. This 'new objectivity' is a stark contrast to his later 'Organisches Bauen' (Organic Building) such as the Philharmonie **49** of 1963. The period between the rise of the Nazis in 1933 and the post-war rebuilding were difficult for Scharoun. Modern architecture, like modern art, was outlawed as being 'degenerate' or 'cultural bolshevism' with the Baupolizei insisting on pitched roofs and a folk vernacular style. With the fifteen or so housing commissions built during this period, there emerges a preoccupation with the internal manipulation of spaces, within an external envelope which, more or less, conforms to the 'Heimatstil'. The Baensch house presents a conventional two-storey split gable to the road but breaks out into a stepped fan form to the private garden at the rear where the double pitch roof is cut back to expose a large first floor roof terrace facing south to the Havel lakes. The complex geometry

of the plan reveals the overlay of several ideas where the central living room is open and spacious containing a careful grouping of elements. Dining space, staircase, piano and conservatory pivot around the central sofa which occupies the internal level change and looks out over the garden terraces to the lake below. These spatial experiments place a greater emphasis on flowing space, closer interrelationships of elements and freer forms, characteristics which re-emerge in Scharoun's post-war public buildings.

145 Three Contemporary Grunewald Villas 1983–84

Furtwänglerstrasse, Wernerstrasse,
Wilmersdorf

Bartels and Schmidt-Ott

At the turn of the century, villa districts were established on the edges of the city. The Grunewald, south-west of the centre and at the end of the Kurfürstendamm, was a rural place with lakes and beech woods. The desire for 'a house in green surroundings' could be realised here in a naturally picturesque landscape with tree-lined avenues, well connected by the Berlin-Potsdam railway. The area today remains much the same, a quiet leafy suburb of large villas in a variety of styles from Italianate to Baroque. The corner site here at Furtwänglerstrasse and Wernerstrasse had been occupied by a large villa which was damaged during the war. Bartels and Schmidt-Ott placed three compact villas on the triangular site around a central garden which retains the simple rural landscape of grass and trees. Like many of the surrounding villas which have been subdivided, each of the new blocks contains a mix of maisonettes and apartments.

Using a variety of Euclidean forms, based loosely on the square, the circle and the triangle, each design incorporates a build-up of floor plans which recognise the different opportunities offered by living on the ground, above the ground or within the roof. Smooth white rendered surfaces, modern fenestration and angular copper roofs, combined with a sympathetic scale, bring a fresh new dimension to the area and continue the established tradition of the neighbouring villas in providing a strong stylistic identity.

Outer suburbs

146 Kreuzkirche (Church of the Cross)
1927–29

Hohenzollerndamm 130a, Schmargendorf, Wilmersdorf

Ernst Paulus, Günther Paulus

In this relatively unknown work, the architects have created an expressionist building of immense power which retains the Gothic spirit. From overall concept to detail design, the work is both impressive and imaginative. An unexpected tension is created by the separation of the tower from the polygonal nave which avoids a collision of form and enhances the identity of each. An extraordinary sculptural quality is achieved by acrobatic brickwork spiralling up the buttresses and zigzagging along the frieze. The entrance porch is crowned by a multi-layered blue glazed ceramic roof in an attempt to compete with the monumentality of the wide tower with its triple spires.

147 Reihenhauser (Terraced Houses) 1925

Schorlemerallee 13–23a, Dahlem, Zehlendorf

Hans Luckhardt, Wassili Luckhardt, Alfons Anker

On its completion the terrace must have presented a strong contrast to the adjacent turn of the century houses. Abstract cubist forms, dark horizontal windows and overlapping planes give a strong geometric rhythm to the row. Plain white staggered surfaces encourage the play of shadows and are reminiscent of the folded paper studies from Josef Albers' preliminary coursework at the Bauhaus. By 1925 the Luckhardt brothers, their roots in the utopian ideals of Bruno Taut's 'Die Gläserne Kette' (the Glass Chain), had moved on to the more rational approach of 'Der Ring' (the Ring Group) which included Mies van der Rohe and Hugo Häring. When faced with the harsh realities of the Weimar Republic, Taut was soon to follow, switching from his pursuit of a glass paradise to that of pioneering social housing co-operatives. Cross-fertilisation of ideas continued between individuals as they worked towards 'Neue Sachlichkeit' (the New Objectivity). At Schorlemeralle, the mannered use of brickwork to delineate attic, window and balcony, can also be found in Taut's Siedlung Britz **130** and Häring's Siedlung Siemensstadt **131**. Together with Alfons Anker, the Luckhardts produced some extraordinary examples of the International Style including an addition to this terrace at Nos 12–12c in 1929 and the villas at Am Rupenhorn **141** in 1928.

148 Haus Wiegand 1911–12

Peter-Lenné-Strasse 28–30, Dahlem,
Zehlendorf

Peter Behrens

If the Turbine Hall for AEG **123**, completed in 1909 by Behrens, served as a modern temple to the machine age, this house completed three years later refers back to more traditional aspects of Greek antiquity. During this period, when Behrens' office was experimenting with new materials and new forms, some of his work was surprisingly neo-Classical. His design for the German Embassy in St Petersburg (1912) employed post and lintol, Doric columns and axial symmetry in a style approved by Kaiser Wilhelm II.

The Wiegand house, however, has a less monumental quality with its domestic scale, asymmetry and portico which engages with the street. A machine-like precision is brought to the construction of the ashlar and an academic rigour to the accurate detailing, appropriately enough for its archaeologist owner Theodor Wiegand. The sharp-edged limestone and stripped Classicism provides an austere physiognomy in contrast to the earlier romantic 'Biedermeier' style providing an historic link between Schinkel, almost a century earlier, and Speer, twenty years later.

149 Freie Universität (Free University) Arts Building 1962–73

Habelschwerdter Allee, Schwendener Strasse,
Dahlem, Zehlendorf

Georges Candilis, Alexis Josic, Shadrach Woods, Manfred Schiedhelm, Jean Prouvé

The political upheaval of 1948 prevented many students from attending Berlin University, then in the Soviet-controlled Eastern sector. The answer was to create a 'free university' of the West in Dahlem where various departments had been based since the 1920s. Many of the departments are still accommodated in rented villas - characteristic of the area - whereas the arts building embodies the spirit of the 1960s with its tapestry-like plan of flexible space. Using a composite structure of steel and reinforced concrete which can be dismantled,

the system can be adapted to meet the varying requirements of corridors, teaching spaces, auditoria and campus atria. Jean Prouvé's engineering artistry was used in detailing modular clip-on cladding panels of Cor Ten steel. Unfortunately, the rusted steel aesthetic has resulted in the nickname of 'Rust Arbour' which together with the proliferation of posters and graffiti contribute towards a rather sad feeling of decay.

Outer suburbs

150 Philosophisches Institut (Philosophy Institute) 1981–83

Habelschwerdter Allee 30, Dahlem, Zehlendorf

Hinrich Baller, Inken Baller

The Ballers have forged a style of their own from Gothic, Gaudi and German expressionism. Their inverted boat roof form - a recurring motif - echoes the Mansard or Baroque roofs of the older buildings. Compared to its larger neighbour, this university building enjoys more success with respect to scale and context while still expressing its modern reinforced concrete structure and large areas of glass. A formality is given to the street frontage by the repetition of symmetrical bays, separated by coupled columns.

This contrasts with the rear where a less formal order enables the architecture to integrate well with a beautiful landscape of grassy hillocks and silver birches. Filigree ironwork balustrading provides a decorative signature to the balconies and romantic bridge link at the rear.

151 Siedlung Onkel-Toms-Hütte (Uncle Tom's Cabin Residential Estate) 1926–31

Argentinische Allee, Riemeisterstrasse, Onkel-Tom-Strasse, Zehlendorf

Bruno Taut, Hugo Häring, Otto Rudolf Salvisberg et al.

This 'forest siedlung' was built in an area of woodland on the outskirts of Zehlendorf and connected to the railway network when the U-Bahn station 'Onkel Toms Hütte' was constructed. Salvisberg's station, completed in 1931, includes a row of shops, post office, restaurant and cinema and provides a 'centre' for the estate. A predominance of 'Zeilenbau' (row housing) and apartment blocks are beautifully integrated into a wooded landscape of pines and silver birches. The housing blocks are kept low in scale - below the height of the trees - and are linked by curved roads and common green spaces. Taut's use of brightly coloured render, shared by Häring and Salvisberg, brings identity and variation to the repetition of the blocks and provides a successful contrast to the surrounding nature. While the apartment blocks each display a separate colour, the 'Zeilenbau' adopt a more subtle ploy. A typical three-storey row will display a colour, such as blue, where each house, along the length of the terrace, is identified by varying the shade or tone of this colour. Only a narrow band of the attic strip is picked out in white serving to unify the row. This pattern is repeated on other rows using quite vivid shades of red, yellow or green. For seventy years this siedlung, along with Britz **130**, has stood as an exemplar for modernist housing. The design proves to be the antithesis of most modernist clichés. Colourful and well detailed, integrated with its surroundings, appreciated by its residents, it also successfully creates a 'sense of place'.

1   *Bruno Taut*
2   *Hugo Häring*
3   *Otto Rudolph Salvisberg*
4   *Hans Poelzig*
5   *Paul Schmitthenner*

152 Haus Otte 1922

Wolzogenstrasse 17, Zehlendorf

Walter Gropius

This design offers an insight to the early work of Gropius, better known for his work with the Bauhaus after its move to Dessau in 1925. Following the First World War, Gropius became director of the Grand Ducal School of Arts and Crafts in Weimar, a post held until the outbreak of war by the Belgian architect Henry van de Velde. In 1919, Gropius formed the Bauhaus when the Academy of Fine Arts was amalgamated with the School of Arts and Crafts in an attempt to break down barriers between the artist and the craftsman. Perhaps some of the ideological conflicts of this early period can be found in the design of the Otte house. In 1921 Gropius built the Sommerfeldt house (later destroyed) nearby for a timber merchant in solid log construction revealing certain influences of Frank Lloyd Wright and the 'Dombauhütte' by Peter Behrens. The façade of the Otte house not only bears a startling resemblance to that of the Sommerfeldt house but carries over influences from van de Velde with its reduced ornament, smooth surfaces and cube-like compactness. Symmetrical façades, pitched roofs and overhanging eaves were soon to give way to the more abstract qualities of 'Neue Sachlichkeit'.

153 Haus Freudenberg 1907–08

Potsdamer Chaussee 48, Nikolassee, Zehlendorf

Hermann Muthesius

In the early 1900s Berlin did not escape the European fashion for country houses. When serving as an attaché to the German Embassy in London, Muthesius had researched English architecture and design at the request of the Kaiser. His ideal model of an Arts and Crafts culture was propagated in his book of 1904, *Das Englische Haus*, before going on, three years later, to become a co-founder of the Deutsche Werkbund. It is interesting, therefore, to view this house against a background of works by C. F. A. Voysey, M. H. Baillie-Scott, Philip Webb, and in particular Edward Prior. The adoption of the butterfly plan, diagonal axis and centralised gable are clearly influenced by 'The Barn' built at Exmouth by Prior in 1897. Muthesius built this house for his friend Hermann Freudenberg in an ideal setting, close to the Wannsee, a year after completing a house for himself on the adjacent site at number 49. While the blend of medieval half-timbering with Arts and Crafts details provides the Freudenberg house with its stylistic identity, it is the geometric assembly of elements which provide it with such a strong sense of presence. Sitting the house into the ground, the diagonal approach, and the weight of the central gable above the small entrance all contribute towards the drama.

Outer suburbs

154 Strandbad Wannsee 1929–30
Strandbadweg 25, Nikolassee, Zehlendorf
Martin Wagner, Richard Ermisch

The area of south-west Berlin enjoys a beautiful landscape of lakes and forests. Lines of communication between the city centre and Potsdam run through Wannsee with Berlin's first railway opening in 1838. A bathing beach was first established here on the edge of Lake Havel in 1907 with a 400 metre long stretch divided by fences to segregate men and women. Such prudery was overcome during the 1920s when a growing awareness of the benefits of sunlight

and fresh air increased the popularity of bathing. The surviving complex of low horizontal pavilions linked by a first-floor walkway and roof terraces was designed by Wagner, who at the time was chief city architect of Berlin, and Ermisch who in 1937 designed the exhibition halls at the Funkturm **134**. The steel framed buildings are clad with terracotta panels and contain changing facilities, shops, cafés and a restaurant. In its heyday, the 1,300 metres of beach could hold 20,000 bathers making it Europe's largest inland open air bathing facility. Tall curved basket seats, characteristic of that period, serve as a present day reminder of sunshine and fun in pre-war Berlin.

155 Pfaueninsel (Peacock Island)

Pfaueninsel, Glienicke and Potsdam

155 Pfaueninsel (Peacock Island) 1793–1816,
1816–34 (illustration opposite, lower)

Wannsee, Berlin

156 Schloss Pfaueninsel 1794–95

Johann Gottlieb David Brendel

157 Kavalierhaus 1824–25

Karl Friedrich Schinkel

Situated in the south-west corner of the Havel
Lakes, the island was developed in two distinct
phases. The first belonged to an era of the
romantic landscaped garden initiated in 1793 by
King Friedrich Wilhelm II and his mistress Gräfin
Lichtenau. Following visits to the Italian isle of
Capri, and inspired by the English use of the
'folly', work started to create the illusion of a wild
island, with a ruined castle, which could be
enjoyed following a boat trip on the lakes. Peacocks had been important decorative additions
to Roman gardens and were also used by early
Christians as symbols of paradise. Their intro-
duction in 1795 gave the island its name and was
followed later by many other exotic animals contributing to the illusion of a wilderness.

The **Schloss Pfaueninsel** of 1794–95 was originally known as the 'Roman Villa'. Johann Gottlieb
David Brendel served as architect, site manager
and contractor with the monarch himself direct-
ing work on occasional visits to the island. Designed to resemble a ruin and constructed largely
of timber, the façade was painted using quartz
sand additives to resemble stonework (restored
in 1974–75 to its original form). The bridge
linking the two towers was originally constructed
of untreated wood and was replaced by a cast
iron filigreed bridge in 1807. By way of a contrast, the interiors are highly refined and beautifully decorated. Extensive use of indigenous wood
is used to create panelled walls and articulated

Schloss Pfaueninsel

The Meierei

pilasters. The position occupied by the Schloss
on the north-west edge of the island enables it to
be seen from the Marble Palace in Potsdam.

At the north-eastern edge of the island, also visible
from the Potsdam approach, sits the **Meierei**
(Dairy) in an open meadow. Designed and constructed by Brendel also in 1794 in the spirit of the
English folly it resembles a ruined priory.

123

Pfaueninsel, Glienicke and Potsdam

The Kavalierhaus

The second phase, from 1816 to 1834, during the reign of Friedrich Wilhelm III and Queen Luise involved significant developments by the landscape architect Peter Joseph Lenné in conjunction with the royal gardener Joachim Anton Ferdinand Fintelmann. It was during this period that Beethoven wrote his 6th symphony, the 'Pastoral'. The landscape was enhanced by axis, vistas, meadows and gardens together with a menagerie, started in 1824, containing a cage for eagles, an ape house, an aviary and a pond for exotic water fowl. Additions four year later included a bear-pit, a kangaroo house and cages for wolves and foxes. Although surrounded by water, the gardens were dependent on an artificial irrigation system driven by machine. A round reservoir located on the island's highest point featured a cast iron fountain resembling a candlestick which produced a light-reflecting cascade: a crystalline water tree.

Karl Friedrich Schinkel collaborated with Lenné in identifying key sites for various constructions in this 'natural' stage-set. The **Kavalierhaus** of 1824–25 was created by Schinkel by combining the façade of a late Gothic house, acquired by Friedrich Wilhem III's eldest son Prince Karl and transported from Danzig, with the tower of an existing guest house completed in 1804. The resulting building with its two castellated towers reflected the appearance of a neo-Gothic English country house.

The Llama House of 1830 (demolished in 1870) was designed by Albert Dietrich Schadow in the Italian villa style combining elements of the Palazzo Caprini and the Casa Cenci. Schadow also supervised the construction of the Palm House of the same year (destroyed by fire in 1880) following a design by Schinkel which combined Indian and

Islamic ornamentation. **Queen Luise's Memorial** in the form of a small Doric temple was constructed in 1829 on a rise at the edge of the trees facing the dairy across the meadow. Schadow utilised a sandstone portico from Queen Luise's Mausoleum in Charlottenburg which was being upgraded. The surviving building serves as a poignant memorial to the Queen, its north-facing Doric façade shaded by a backdrop of greenery.

The artistic development of the island effectively ended in 1840 following the death of the monarch. Realising that the growing popularity of the menagerie with the public was becoming a threat to the island, the new monarch, Friedrich Wilhelm IV, donated the animals to the newly established Berlin Zoo **32**. In 1924 the island was declared a nature reserve, but insufficient care during and after the war years resulted in paths being shifted, gardens altered and viewing points being overgrown. Today much of the illusion remains: the tranquil, pastoral scene interrupted audibly by the haunting cries of the peacocks.

Queen Luise's Memorial

158 Park Klein-Glienicke 1816–22, 1824–50
Königstrasse, Wannsee, Zehlendorf

Peter Joseph Lenné

During the late eighteenth century, the architectural move from Baroque to Classical was complimented by a landscaping move from French geometric order to a freer English model. Nowhere was this marriage of styles better exploited than in the collaborative works of Karl Friedrich Schinkel and Peter Joseph Lenné.

In 1824 Prince Karl, eldest son of King Friedrich Wilhelm III acquired Klein-Glienicke from Prince von Hardenberg and commissioned Lenné to create a landscaped park. Lenné counteracted its small scale by interconnecting a variety of desolate areas, each opening out to offer vistas over the surrounding countryside. This pattern is overlaid with a concept of woodlands which extends from the denser evergreens in the north to the more open deciduous trees in the south. Schinkel succeeds in fusing a variety of buildings with the landscape to create an aesthetic delight. Together with his gifted associate, Ludwig Persius (1803–45), he sought to express the harmonious coexistence of man and nature. A further opportunity to embellish the Potsdam landscape was given to Schinkel and Persius on the Babelsberg estate, immediately to the south of Klein-Glienicke. A **summer residence** for Prince Wilhelm, Prince Karl's brother, was built in a Tudor-Gothic style. Viewed across the lake from the Glienicke Bridge **162**, the towers and battlements of this late Romantic castle provide the architectural accent to this southern view.

159 Schloss Glienicke 1824–27

Karl Friedrich Schinkel

The estate, under the previous ownership of Prince von Hardenberg, had included a mansion house as a summer residence. When the property was bought by Prince Karl, the building was reconstructed and enlarged by Schinkel to include a garden courtyard, stable block and bell tower. The enthusiasm for classical antiquity is apparent in the combination of Italian vernacular planning, Renaissance forms and Greek details. The symmetrical palace façade is modest in its scale and restrained in its articulation, facing south over an open meadow. The assemblage of buildings is linked by a series of gardens, formal and enclosed or informal and open, containing sculpture and fountains. Fragments from Roman and Greek antiquity, many recovered during visits abroad, are used to embellish the buildings or are half-buried strategically in the ground awaiting 'discovery'.

160 Kasino 1824–25

Karl Friedrich Schinkel

The casino, or ornamental pavilion, was built on the site of an old billiard hall looking out over the lake to the north and the park to the south. The design is based on an Italian villa and Schinkel, having just returned from an Italian visit, illustrated his drawings of the building to include the royal party arriving by gondolas. From the shore a series of ascending gardens lead to stairs under the cover of pergolas which extend to either side of the building. The simple rectangular two-storey forms provide a backdrop for the ornamentation of flower urns, bronze statues and the flanking pergolas which frame the views over the lake.

161 Grosse Neugierde (Large Curiosity)
1835–3

Karl Friedrich Schinkel

In the late eighteenth century, the previous owner of the Glienicke estate had built a small pavilion enfronting the recently established main road between Potsdam and Berlin. Unobserved, he would spy on the passers-by and appropriately named his little structure 'Curiosity'. Prince Karl, whilst also sharing an interest in his predecessor's pastime, preferred to celebrate the act in a more formal way by installing his own 'Large Curiosity'. Taking the form of a circular temple, Schinkel based the design on the Choragic Monument of Lysikrates in Athens. The peristyle of sixteen Corinthian columns sits high above the ground on a solid cylindrical podium, above the heads of passers-by. This vantage point offered panoramic views, not only of the road but also of the stone arched bridge built by Schinkel (later destroyed) and the distant views of Potsdam over the Havel.

162 Glienicker Brücke 1905–07
Crosses the Havel/Glienicker Lake,
Königstrasse, Wannsee/Potsdam

The first bridge, constructed in wood in 1662
formed a link between Potsdam and the Elector's hunting grounds in Klein-Glienicke **158**. It
was not until 1793 that this became the main
route to Berlin, travellers having previously
crossed by the Lange Brücke and through the
Teltower Vorstadt. In 1836 the wooden bridge
was replaced by a more solid construction of
stone arches. The design by Karl Friedrich
Schinkel was stylistically sympathetic to his
repertoire of constructions in the adjacent Park
Klein-Glienicke. The present steel suspension
bridge resulted from the increase of road traffic at the turn of the century together with a
requirement to allow the passage of larger
ships. Blown up in 1945 and rebuilt in 1950,
the bridge served as a crossing point between
East and West throughout the era of the Berlin
Wall. During this period, the symmetry of the

simple suspension structure was visually bisected by each side painting their half a different hue of grey-green. The dividing line in the
middle often became the scene for the exchange of spies.

Potsdam

Early references to Poztupimi (Potsdam) appear in documents dated 993 when the Emperor Otto III passed on ownership rights to his
aunt, Abbess Mathilde von Quedlinburg. Its
strategic importance dates from 1150 when
Albrecht the Bear, Margrave of Nordmark, first
secured the Havel crossing. It was not until the
thirteenth century, however, that a settlement
of any real size was established.

During the reign of Friedrich Wilhelm, the
Great Elector (1640–88) Berlin underwent major
developments of new fortifications and the establishment of new districts. These new initiatives
reached as far as Potsdam, when in 1660 Friedrich
Wilhelm employed Johann Gregor Memhardt to
lay out a new residence in the town on the banks
of the Havel. This set a pattern for the following
Elector, Friedrich III, who became the first King of
Prussia in 1701, and the subsequent kings to
continue the development of Potsdam into a
cultural metropolis with a European reputation.
Berlin, with its royal residence and city palaces,
was the administrative capital of Prussia but
Potsdam, only a short journey away, offered an
escape, a life apart in idyllic surroundings. The

Neue Orangerie, Sanssouci

Pfaueninsel, Glienicke and Potsdam

natural beauty of the River Havel, various lakes fringed with forests and flat stretches of meadow provided a varied landscape for the recreation of the court. Friedrich Wilhelm I (the Soldier King) concentrated more on extending the town to accommodate his soldiers, laying out fortifications and creating a garrison town. A more artistic emphasis returned when in 1745 King Friedrich II (Frederick the Great), instigated the construction of a summer palace in the grounds of Sanssouci. By the end of the eighteenth century, Potsdam had become a place of royal houses and gardens enclosed behind protective walls. Territorial expansion outwith Potsdam followed in 1783 with King Friedrich Wilhelm II's creation of the Neuer Garten with the Marmorpalais (Marble Palace) by the shores of the Heiliger See, a small lake connected to the Havel by a short canal. The Cecilienhof, a large country house in the English style, was built nearby in 1916 for Crown Prince Wilhelm of Prussia. It was here that the Potsdam Agreement was reached by Truman, Stalin and Attlee in August 1945. Friedrich Wilhelm III also focused his interest on rural Potsdam, in particular with the Pfaueninsel (Peacock Island) 155 on the Havel.

Potsdam also developed as a manufacturing town producing cloth, glass, guns, ships and tobacco goods, becoming the seat of local government from 1809. The opening of the Potsdam-Berlin railway in 1838, the first in the region, established further links between the two centres with Potsdam remaining a permanent residence of the Hohenzolern rulers until 1913. At the very end of the Second World War, the Baroque town centre was destroyed by heavy bombing. Rebuilding began in 1958 with the Communist regime favouring precast concrete system building which sits oddly juxtaposed with the remaining Baroque.

163 Altes Rathaus (Old Town Hall)
1753–55
Am Alten Markt 1–2, Potsdam
Johann Boumann, Carl Ludwig Hildebrandt

The Town Hall was built as part of King Friedrich II's grand plan for Potsdam which also included the palace 177 and park at Sanssouci 176. The site had been occupied by a medieval council building and the old market square, which was redesigned in the style of a Roman piazza. Johann Boumann's inspiration for the Rathaus was an unbuilt project by Palladio for the Palazzo Angarano in Vincenza. Although relatively small in scale, the main façade expresses the building's grand status by its series of Corinthian columns, large entablature, and attica with sculpted figures. Above the entrance, the attica is capped by a cartouche displaying the town arms of Potsdam, and the central domed tower is crowned by a gilded figure of Atlas. Badly damaged in 1945, the building was restored between 1963 and 1966.

The Obelisk in the centre of the Alten Markt was originally erected in 1753–55 by Georg Wenzeslaus von Knobelsdorff.

164 Nikolaikirche (Nikolai Church)
1830–37

Am Alten Markt, Potsdam

*Karl Friedrich Schinkel, Ludwig Persius,
Friedrich August Stüler*

The dome of the Nikolaikirche is the focal point of Potsdam, a landmark of the flat Havel landscape, visible from afar. The visual treatment of the cylindrical section with the pilasters sitting above a colonnade is reminiscent of St Paul's Cathedral in London by Wren and the Pantheon in Paris by Soufflot, both visited by Schinkel in 1826. Domed buildings held a special place in Schinkel's design proposals - continuing a line established by Brunelleschi, Bramante and Michelangelo - with this being the only one built. Unfortunately, Schinkel died before its completion but having prepared a design to the approval of King Friedrich Wilhelm III in such a way that a dome could later be added. Ludwig Persius built the original design with a double-pitched roof and portico in 1830–37. Following the King's death in 1840 and with the support of King Friedrich Wilhelm IV, the dome was added by Friedrich August Stüler in 1843–49. The four corner bell towers were added as buttresses against the thrust of the dome. Extensive war damage was repaired up until 1975 and the building was rededicated in 1981.

165 'Acht-Ecken-Haus' (Eight Cornered House)
1771

Friedrich-Ebert-Strasse 122, Potsdam

Karl von Gontard

This is the sole survivor of four identical town houses, three of which were destroyed during the Second World War. Originally planned around a crossroads, inscribing the corners of the blocks created a small eight-sided square which was once a delightful example of Baroque planning. Each chamfered corner contained a beautifully detailed entrance door and first-floor balcony with wrought-iron railings. The remaining example reveals a curved balcony supported by a sculpted bracket and the arched French window access capped by a cartouche. The four blocks were thereby tied together by a diagonal symmetry across the corners. The surviving block, restored in 1956, now sits somewhat forlornly on the edge of the widened Friedrich-Ebert-Strasse.

Pfaueninsel, Glienicke and Potsdam

166 Marstall (Royal Stables), now Film Museum
1685

Karl-Liebknecht-Forum 1, Potsdam

Johann Arnold Nering, Andreas Ludwig Krüger

Originally constructed by Nering in 1685 as an orangerie, the building incorporated an earlier garden portal on the northern side reputedly designed by Johann Gregor Memhardt. The conversion to royal stables was executed by Andreas Ludwig Krüger in 1746 to a design by Georg Wenzeslaus von Knobelsdorff. This work also included the addition of an upper half storey and an extension to the west, making it over 130 metres long. Projecting portals, capped by sculpture, were added to the narrow east and west gables. The long southern façade was articu-

lated by two projecting pavilions, each with their attica decorated by sandstone figures of horses and riders. The building was restored in 1977–80 by the Polish State Department of Ancient Monuments and has been used as a film museum since 1982.

167 Havelkolonnade des Stadtschlosses (Havel Colonnades) 1745–46, 1969

Am Karl-Liebknecht-Forum, Potsdam

Georg Wenzeslaus von Knobelsdorff

Following the completion of the Interhotel in 1969 by Weber, Töpfer and Gödicke, various works were carried out to the adjacent plaza and spaces connecting the pier on the banks of the Havel. Significant elements recovered from the ruined Stadtschloss, demolished in 1961, were used to construct a colonnade along the main route between the hotel and the pier. This, perhaps, may be regarded as a modern equivalent of their original purpose to connect the palace with the stables. The fine detailing of the sandstone columns, entablature and parapet by Knobelsdorff is further enhanced by the incorporation of various fine sculptures by Friedrich Christian Glume, Georg Franz Ebenhech, Johann August Nahl, Johann Gottlieb Heymüller and Johann Peter Benckert.

168 168 Hiller-Brandtsche Häuser 1769

Breite Strasse (formerly Wilhelm-Külz-Strasse) 26–27, Potsdam

Georg Christian Unger

Part of King Friedrich II's grand plan for Potsdam, these imposing twin town houses were designed to present a palace façade to Breite Strasse, at that time used as a ceremonial route. Built for the merchant Johann Friedrich Hiller and the tailor Johann Gerhard Brandt, the two three-storey corner blocks are linked by a two-storey central section which was used to billet the military. The design by Georg Christian Unger, influenced by Inigo Jones' design for Whitehall Palace of 1619 in London, displays generous proportions and palatial pretensions. Sculpted figures from Ro- man mythology align the parapets of both houses and stand guard above the twin entrances of the central section. The high degree of modelling and detail articulation is highlighted by the recent rein- statement of the original colour scheme of yellow-ochre pilasters, cornices and window surrounds set against a background of dark red stucco.

169 Pumpwerk (Pumphouse) 1841–42

Zeppelin Strasse (Leninallee) 176, Potsdam

Ludwig Persius

This remarkable monument to the early years of German engineering was built to house the pump which served the fountains and water systems of Sanssouci park. With a high awareness of the picturesque, perhaps even the surreal, Persius adopts the form of an oriental mosque resplend-ent in all its Moorish ornament reflected in the waters of the Havelbucht. The façades are con-structed with turquoise and white glazed bricks and the minaret conceals the chimney. The steam engine was built in 1841 by the Borsig Engineer-ing firm **110** - still in existence in Berlin today - and was fully renovated in 1985.

170 Alte Wache (Old Guardhouse) 1795–97

Otto-Nuschke-Strasse 45, Potsdam

Andreas Ludwig Krüger

Occupying a corner site on the edge of the first Baroque new town, the old guardhouse replaced an earlier gatehouse dating from the time of King Friedrich Wilhelm I (the Soldier King). During the late eighteenth century, King Friedrich II contin-ued with improvements to the town, displaying preference for ancient, Roman and classical themes. Krüger based his design on Carl Gotthard Langhans' Mohrenkolonnaden completed in Ber-lin ten years earlier. The two main façades con-sist entirely of two-storey arched colonnades on coupled columns. The parapet was decorated with the sculptures of ancient gods, such as Mars and Bellona, a reference to the building's military purpose.

Pfaueninsel, Glienicke and Potsdam

171 Zweite Barocke Neustadt (Second Baroque Expansion) 1732–42

Brandenburger Strasse, Potsdam

Ingenieurkapitän Berger, Peter von Gayette

The second Baroque expansion of the town dates from the reign of Friedrich Wilhelm I, laid out by the military engineer, Captain Berger, with Brandenburger Strasse forming a central east-west axis. Starting in the west at the Brandenburg Gate, constructed later in 1769, the predominately right-angled street pattern is occasionally cut obliquely by the earlier streets laid out by the Elector in 1668. The resultant gridiron re-formed the district into twenty-one new blocks or quarters. The buildings enfronting the streets were predominately of two storeys with the horizontal eaves line topped by regular dormers or broken by an occasional three-storey façade. The architect, Peter von Gayette, relies on varying a series of repetitive house types to give each street a different identity. Further variation was achieved by changing the colour of the stucco. At present, enough of the original houses remain to convey the atmosphere created by the small-scale street frontages and Baroque town plan.

172 172 Nauener Tor (Nauen Gate) 1755

Hegelalle, Friedrich-Ebert-Strasse, Potsdam

Johann Gottfried Büring

The town gates of Potsdam expressed a variety of architectural styles. The Neustadt Gate (1753) by Georg Wenzeslaus von Knobelsdorff contains two Egyptian-style obelisks. Both the Berlin Gate (1753) by Johann Boumann and the Brandenburg Gate (1770) by Karl von Gontard and Georg Christian Unger, are based on the Roman triumphal arch. The Nauen Gate, however, represents the first example outside England of the Gothic Revival style. Büring collaborated closely with King Friedrich II (Frederick the Great), who not only commissioned the work but also produced sketches for the design. The twin towers are flanked by colonnaded wings which open their arcaded sides to the town. A closer inspection will reveal the sculpted masques on the arched piers by Benjamin Giese.

173 Holländisches Viertel (Dutch Quarter)
1732–42

Mittelstrasse, Benkertstasse, Potsdam

Johann Boumann

Four of the twenty-one blocks to the north-east of the second Baroque expansion **171** made up the Dutch quarter containing in total 134 houses. The decision by King Friedrich Wilhelm I to bring the carpenter Johann Boumann from Amsterdam to supervise construction proved controversial. The Dutch immigrants brought with them their own style of brick gabled town houses which were out of context with Berger and Gayette's Baroque. Variations were introduced consisting of terraced houses with eaves to the street and a detached house type with hipped roofs, but the three window wide gable type proliferates. Perhaps because of its position on the edge of the new town, the Dutch quarter has survived more intact than other blocks to the west. The first phase of a five-year restoration programme was started in 1972 and the final phase, started in 1984, was completed in 1993.

174 Hauptpost (Post Office Headquarters)
1897–1900

Berliner Strasse (formerly Heinrich-Rau-Allee), Potsdam

Hacker

Although built during the time of Kaiser Wilhelm II and displaying an imperial scale, the style of the Post Office Headquarters refers more to the earlier Wilhelmian period of the Kings of Prussia. With his design, Hacker conveys more of an institutional feel, not as Imperialistic as the Reichstag **26** of 1894 by Paul Wallot, nor as megalomaniac as the Viktoria Insurance Headquarters **88** of 1913 by Wilhelm Walther. The 'palace' form, emphasised by the projecting corner pavilions and pedimented central entrance portico, is handled with assurance and demonstrates a fine sense of proportion. The details all continue the neo-Baroque theme with the large cartouche within the pediment presumably displaying the post office emblem. As was originally intended, the building still closes the vista north from the Alten Markt, but unfortunately it now has to compete with the adjacent concrete system-built apartment blocks.

175 Einsteinturm (Einstein Tower) 1920–24

Albert-Einstein-Strasse, Telegrafenberg, Potsdam

Erich Mendelsohn

Mendelsohn's quest to create a new architecture without precedent is realised here in this his most powerful construction. It was Albert Einstein's assistant, Erwin Finlay-Freundlich, who instigated the project for an astronomical tower with a specific function in astrophysical research. Light from the cosmos is captured by the upper telescope, projected downwards and reflected by mirror horizontally on to the spectrographic apparatus in the basement laboratory. The building's function, therefore, is very precise: to test by practical experiments Einstein's theory of relativity. Mendlesohn's fascination with the cosmos had been explored earlier in a series of visionary sketches produced in 1917 while serving in the trenches at the Russian Front. In these bold, broadbrush sketches, inspired by Bach's 'Magnificat', the evolution of the form suggests a frantic inclination towards the fantastic. The sculptural composition balances the dynamic play of sweeping vertical and horizontal curves with rhythms of raised and recessed surfaces. At the same time the static condition is achieved by employing a solid base and symmetrical plan. Visual comparisons are somehow unavoidable: nautical machinery, expressionist sculpture or perhaps some

mysterious prehistoric monster with the surface of the building appearing like a taut skin.

It was originally intended that the construction would demonstrate the plastic qualities of concrete as a new material, but difficulties with shuttering necessitated the use of rendered brickwork for the main body of the tower. The expertise of shipwrights was called upon to assist with draughting techniques for the hundreds of complex dimensions required. *In situ*, the building appears smaller and less aggressive than in photographs and remains Mendelsohn's greatest challenge to the 'rectangular mentality'.

176 Sanssouci (Park with Palaces and Gardens) 1740–1860

The park, covering a total area of 290 hectares on the western edge of Potsdam, was developed over two building periods. King Friedrich II (Frederick the Great), began preparations for building the Sanssouci Palace **177**, its terraced vineyard and the eastern garden with the picture gallery at the beginning of his reign in 1740. Further smaller initiatives culminated in 1769 with the completion of the Neues Palais **180** with its deer park further to the west. King Friedrich Wilhelm III concentrated his efforts on the nearby Pfaueninsel **155** and otherwise found much of his enterprise curtailed by the war with Napoleon.

The second period began in 1826 with King Friedrich Wilhelm III's son, Prince Friedrich Wilhelm commissioning Schinkel to convert the Schloss Charlottenhof **181** into a summer residence. Another commission followed three years later in this southern sector for the Court

Gardener's House and Roman Baths **182**, regarded as one of Schinkel's best works. Further acquisitions of the Lindstedt estate to the north-west by the Prince resulted in the Schloss Lindstedt, a modest isolated residence designed for his retirement but not completed until after his death in 1861. Two major buildings were added to the original park by the Prince after his accession to the throne in 1840: the Friedenskirche **184** and the Neue Orangerie **183**.

The first period was essentially Baroque with its symmetrical façades, axial planning and long avenues. The second period involved more picturesque settings for an architecture of Romantic Classicism.

177 Schloss Sanssouci (Sanssouci Palace)
1745–47

Zur historischen Mühle, Sanssouci, Potsdam

Georg Wenzeslaus von Knobelsdorff

King Friedrich II conceived the idea of a palatial retreat outside Potsdam in 'delightful surroundings' involving himself in the design of the project for a year before work started in 1745. The siting of the palace on top of a 'desolate hill' was beautifully exploited by the creation of six curved vineyard terraces. Carefully designed sheltered enclosures to the rear of the south-facing terraces were planted with vines, peaches and apricots. A grand stairway of sweeping curved sections links the palace, down through the terraces to the pond encircled by statues at the foot of the hill. The fountain, originally planned for the pond, had to wait for the construction of the Pump House **169** nearly a century later. The Palace, regarded as one of the best examples of German Rococo, is decorated by the paintings of Adolf von Menzel. The single-storey façade, with its circular domed central section, is heavily decorated by sculpted figures sitting aloft pedestal pilasters between the arched windows. In these surroundings the King could relax 'sans souci' (without cares).

178 Grosse Bildergalerie (Great Picture Gallery) 1755–63

Schopenhauerstrasse, Sanssouci, Potsdam

Johann Gottfried Büring

Flanking the Sanssouci Palace are two additional buildings which continue the Rococo theme. To the west lies the Neue Kammern (New Chambers) built in 1747 by Knobelsdorff originally as an orangerie, then converted into a guest house in 1775 by Karl von Gontard and Georg Christian Unger. Balancing this ensemble to the east is the Great Picture Gallery which represented a grand departure from the normal tradition of incorporating painting collections into the Palace. Sculpted figures from the arts and sciences give the building its

sense of purpose and it remains today the earliest surviving German museum building. The original stock of Italian and Flemish masters were transferred in 1830 to Schinkel's new museum **10** in Berlin. The terrace and 'Dutch Garden' to the south were laid out by Joachim Ludwig Heydert in 1764–66.

Pfaueninsel, Glienicke and Potsdam

179 Chinesisches Teehaus (Chinese Teahouse)
1754–57
Ökonomieweg, Sanssouci, Potsdam
Johann Gottfried Büring

The Teahouse was located at the south-eastern corner of what was then the deer and pheasant park. Royalty led the eighteenth century fascination with all things oriental by amassing collections of artefacts and incorporating a 'Chinese room' into many palaces. This extraordinary structure has a surreal quality, highly decorated with oriental figures and motifs. The circular plan encompasses covered terraces and a centrally domed room incorporating collections of Japanese and Chinese porcelain. The free flowing curved copper roof appears to be both propped up and tied down by lavishly detailed columns. The lantern is crowned by a gilded mandarin by Benjamin Giese and Friedrich Jury expressing both the joy and delight of this 'Tea Temple'.

180 Neues Palais 1763–69
Am Neuen Palais, Sanssouci, Potsdam
Johann Gottfried Büring, Karl von Gontard

Earlier plans to expand the park to the west finally took shape with the building of a New Palace terminating a new 2.5 kilometre long east-west axis which cuts across the north-south axis of Sanssouci Palace **177**. The imposing scale of the new residential palace reflects both the ambitions of Frederick the Great and the status of his new Prussia. Unlike the more modest Sanssouci, the proposals here demonstrate an acute awareness of the grandeur displayed at Versailles and Schönbrunn. Behind the 213 metre long façade are 200 rooms, including a theatre decorated in Rococo style under the direction of von Gontard. Over 400 figures from classical mythology, the work of twelve sculptors, decorate the terrace, court and parapets. The large squat dome sits uncomfortably above the central section, reminiscent of the Prussian 'Pickelhaube' helmet. To the rear, the building looks over a large ceremonial court to a symmetrical ensemble of two additional palace buildings linked by a triumphal arch and semi-circular colonnade. These two identical buildings continue the elevational articulation of the main building with the addition of plinths, porticos and curved sweeping staircases. Corinthian columns and projecting pediments provide a stronger modelling than the main building with its repetitive pattern of alternating window and pilaster. The ensemble forms a memorable example of Baroque planning and provides a grandiose architectural backdrop to the western end of the park.

On the edge of the quadrants to the east of the palace are two small round temples. The **Antikentempel and the Freundschaftstempel** (1768) were built by von Gontard after designs by Frederick the Great inspired by the Temple of Apollo.

181 Schloss Charlottenhof 1826–28
Geschwister-Scholl-Strasse, Sanssouci,
Potsdam
Karl Friedrich Schinkel, Ludwig Persius

The southern expansion of Sanssouci dates from 1826 when King Friedrich Wilhelm III bought the Charlottenhof estate for his son, Crown Prince Friedrich Wilhelm. The Crown Prince indulged his interest in architecture as a willing patron in a successful collaboration with Schinkel and Lenné. The Charlottenhof Palace was constructed out of an existing house occupied originally by the Potsdam architects Boumann, Büring and Gontard. In the rebuilding, Schinkel retained only the battered walls of the basement to create a beautiful Italianate villa with many eclectic details. The royal enthusiasm for Italian antiquity was shared by Schinkel who had returned from his second visit just two years earlier. The rectangular plan is expanded into a cruciform by the intersection of a temple form to provide an entrance portico to the west and a garden portico to the east. Schinkel sets the main entrance doors within antae derived from the Choragic Monument of Thrasyllus in Athens, a recurring source of influence to his work. The garden entrance with its Greek Doric tetrastyle portico leads to bridges over the basement court to address the raised garden with its pergola, fountain, water course and curved tented garden seat. The planning involves axis and counter axis, symmetry and asymmetry, in a picturesque composition of views and vistas clearly illustrated by Schinkel in his design drawings. The interiors are richly decorated in vivid colours and varied themes including influences gleaned from the study of Pompeii.

182 Hofgärtnerei/Römische Bäder (Court Gardener's House/Roman Baths) 1829–35

Lennéstrasse, Sanssouci, Potsdam

Karl Friedrich Schinkel, Ludwig Persius

Following the work at Charlottenhof **181**, the Crown Prince Friedrich Wilhelm commissioned Schinkel to build the Court Gardener's House, later called the Roman Baths, near Charlottenhof in the southern sector of the park. Schinkel's genius as a romantic-artist-architect is demonstrated here in this most sublime work. The ensemble, arranged around an Italianate villa, combines elements of classical and vernacular architecture into a painterly composition. A sequence of volumes and spaces overlap and intersect, inviting the user to enter, discover and enjoy. The central garden court is accessed by passing under a pergola of small columns supporting a foliage roof and entering through an open arch next to the tower. Three sides of the court contain disparate elements while the fourth opens to a small lake with a system of canals. The garden façade of the villa is extended by a pergola which is terminated by a teahouse in the form of a Roman temple. The third side is bordered by an open arched loggia which would be glazed in winter to protect the orange trees. Schinkel creates a sense of organic unity between buildings, constructions, sculptures and nature. A series of comfortable rooms, quiet resting places and open spaces with beautiful views create a picturesque environment where the royal proprietor could enjoy the 'country life'. As at Schloss Glienicke **159** and Schloss Charlottenhof **181**, Ludwig Persius assisted Schinkel in executing the works.

183 Neue Orangerie 1851–60

An der Orangerie, Sanssouci, Potsdam
*Ludwig Persius, Friedrich August Stüler,
Ludwig Ferdinand Hesse*

One of King Friedrich Wilhelm IV's unrealised projects for the estate consisted of a Roman style triumphal way, with a memorial temple for Friedrich II. Starting in 1834, both Schinkel and Persius worked on unrealised designs which grew in scale over the years, culminating in Italian High Renaissance. Work on the avenue finally began a year after Schinkel's death in 1842 only to be curtailed three years later following the death of Persius. A further six years passed before the King resurrected part of the project, having abandoned the avenue and appointing Stüler and Hesse to build the New Orangerie. A monumental stair system rises up through terraces of sculpture to a grand terrace with its geometric sequence of ponds and fountains. The 330 metre long south façade exceeds that of the Neues Palais **180** with the arched colonnades of the end pavilions controlling and framing the vistas to east and west. The palatial scale with formal symmetries incorporates arched openings, colonnades and

flat-roofed towers reminiscent of the Villa Medici or Villa Doria Pamphili in Rome. The central section contains a gallery with the Raphael Room containing a collection of Italian Renaissance masters. A statue of Friedrich Wilhelm IV by Gustav Bläser stands on a pedestal framed by the central arch of the entrance.

184 Friedenskirche (Peace Church) 1845–54

Am Grünen Gitter, Sanssouci, Potsdam

*Ludwig Persius, Ludwig Ferdinand Hesse,
Ferdinand von Arnim*

King Friedrich Wilhelm IV, the former Crown Prince, continued his architectural pursuits after ascending to the throne in 1840. Collaborating with Persius, who became the royal architect following Schinkel's death in 1841, the King's Italian influences were once again brought into play with the Friedenskirche. The early basilican form is derived from San Clemente in Rome and the campanile refers to Santa Maria in Cosmedin. This theme is continued by adopting the Italianate villa form for the school and priest's house. Although the assembly makes a convincing set-piece within itself, it sits uncomfortably out of context among the trees and waterways of the park. The church was started in 1845 to celebrate the first centenary of Sanssouci and following Persius' death in the same year the work was executed by Hesse and von Arnim.

Author's Acknowledgements

I should like to thank the following individuals and organisations for their help in preparing this guide: Douglas Cruickshank and Stuart Renton for their assistance with photographs; Annette Williamson for word processing; Susan Eyre and Andrea Matheson for help with photographic printing; Andrea Faed and Rebecca Smith for assistance with drawing plans; Gudrun Hamacher and the IBA Archiv Berlin for information and drawings; McLaren Murdoch & Hamilton architects for their support and resources; and The Department of Architecture, Edinburgh College of Art for its support, resources and continued encouragement. A special thanks must also be given to the T. Bowhill-Gibson Bequest.

Illustration Credits

The photgraphs are by the author with the assistance of Douglas Cruikshank and Stuart Renton, with the exception of photographs 104, and 108 which are by Armin Röse. The Town Plan on page 11 is reproduced with the kind permission of Landesarchiv, Berlin.

Pergola, Hofgärtnerei/Römische Bäder 182

Index

Index

Index

Index

Map A old town centre and northern Friedrichstadt

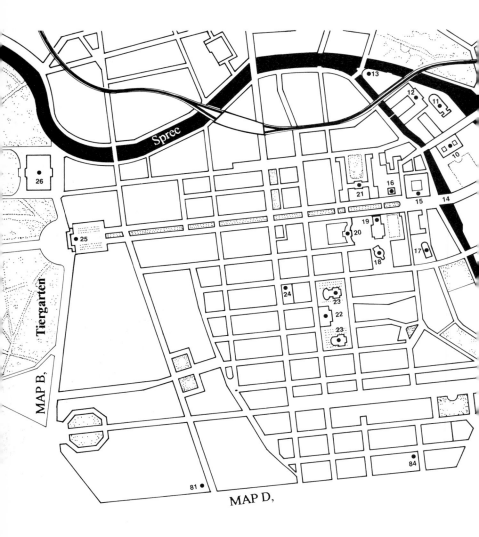

Spree

Tiergarten

MAP B,

MAP D,

0   1000m

N

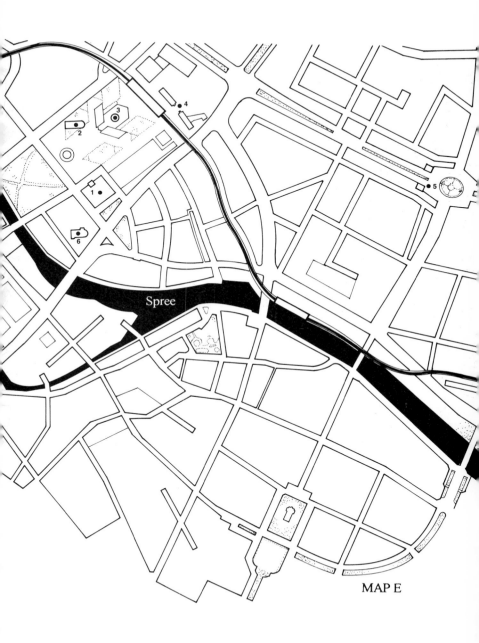

Spree

MAP E

Map B new western centre and Tiergarten

0   1000m   2km

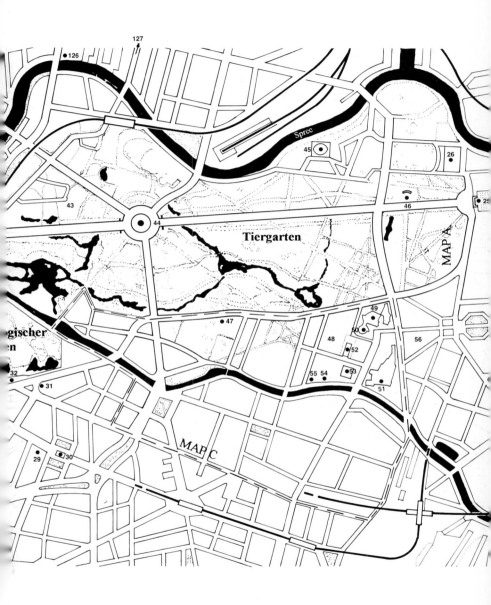

Tiergarten

Spree

MAP A

MAP C

gischer
en

Map C IBA southern Tiergarten

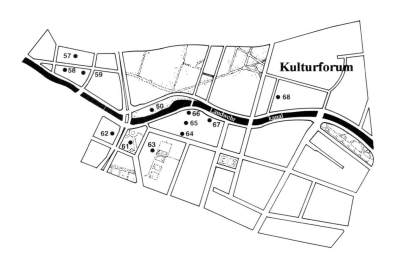

Map D IBA southern Friedrichstadt

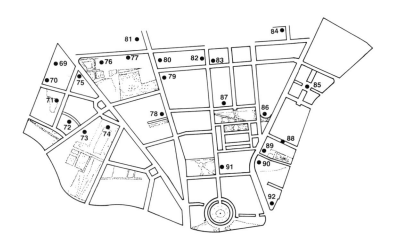

Map E IBA Luisenstadt, SO36

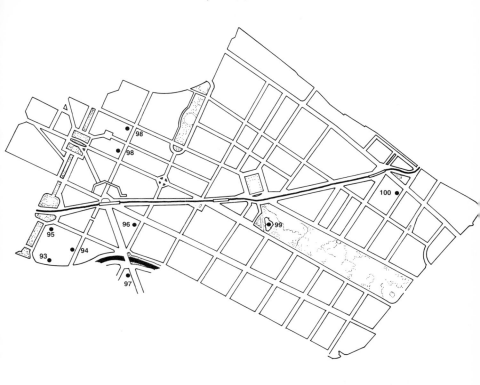

Map F IBA Prager Platz

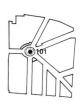

Map G IBA Tegel

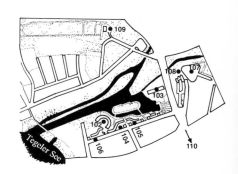

Map H Berlin suburbs

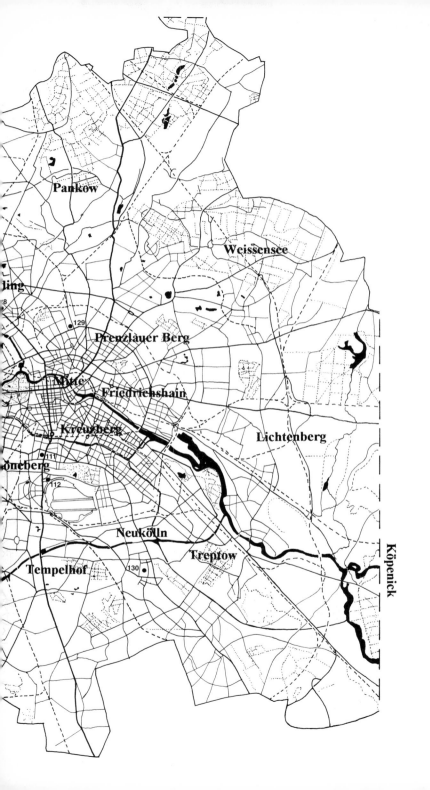

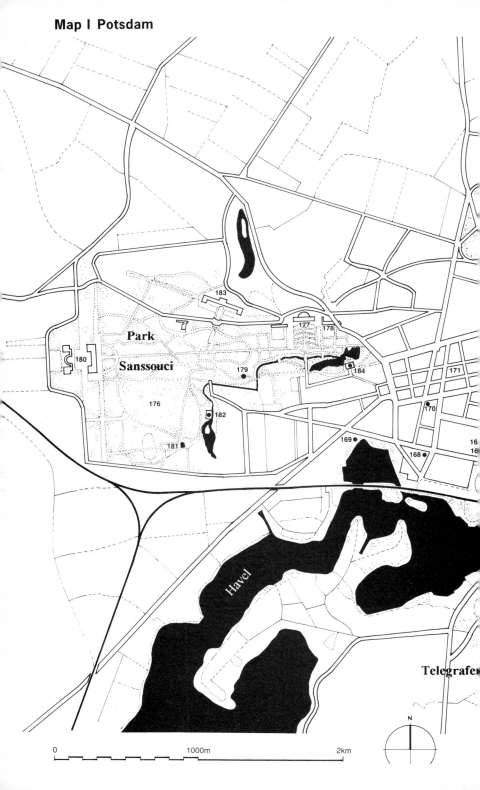

Map I Potsdam

Park

Sanssouci

Havel

Telegrafe

N

0   1000m   2km

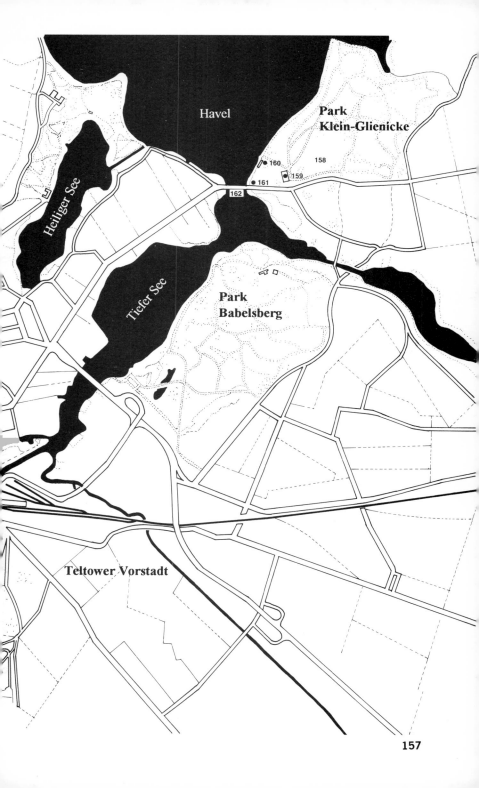

Havel

Park
Klein-Glienicke

Heiliger See

158

160

159

161

162

Tiefer See

Park
Babelsberg

Teltower Vorstadt